The Making of a (PARDONED) Felon During the Civil Rights Movement in America

The Making of a (PARDONED) Felon During the Civil Rights Movement in America

The Physician Who Helped Heal American Democracy

William G. Anderson, DO, FACOS

©2025 All Rights Reserved. No portion of this book may be reproduced, stored in a retrieval system, or transmitted in any form or by any means—electronic, mechanical, photocopy, recording, scanning, or other—except for brief quotations in critical reviews or articles without the prior permission of the author or the American Osteopathic Foundation, Inc.

Published by Game Changer Publishing

Paperback ISBN: 978-1-966659-80-8

Hardcover ISBN: 978-1-966659-81-5

Digital ISBN: 978-1-966659-82-2

www.GameChangerPublishing.com

www.GameChangerPublishing.com

Dedication

I dedicate this book to my wife, Norma, who preceded me to her heavenly home. Without her, my life would not have been the same, and my course would have been significantly altered.

And, to those who have brought joy and meaning to my life over the years —family, friends, colleagues, and patients—you have helped make these stories possible.

And to the American Osteopathic Foundation, my trusted philanthropic partner, who helped me bring this book to life.

And finally, to all of the past, current, and future William G. Anderson Scholars —I dedicate this book to you and to the future of the Osteopathic profession.

The Making of a (PARDONED) Felon During the Civil Rights Movement in America

The Physician Who Helped Heal American Democracy

William G Anderson, DO, FACOS

About this Book

The Making of a [Pardoned] Felon During the Civil Rights Movement in America shines a light on the life of Dr. William G. Anderson, who rose to national prominence as the president of the Albany Movement, the first mass movement in the modern American civil rights era. A distinguished Osteopathic physician, surgeon, educator, and hospital administrator, he tells his story to bear witness to history and inspire a new generation of students and scholars. All proceeds from this book help fund the American Osteopathic Foundation's William G. Anderson, DO, Educational Scholarship Program that aids Osteopathic medical students who have faced societal barriers and who wish to serve disenfranchised populations.

Foreword
by Pat Grauer

"I was about eight," she said, "a little Negro girl walking alone down the sidewalk along my street in Atlanta. Suddenly, there were about forty Ku Klux Klansmen, in full regalia and in full daylight, marching toward me."

I was interviewing Norma Anderson for the first time, and I could feel the gooseflesh rising on my arms. "You must have been terrified," I said.

She looked at me quizzically, as if fear had not occurred to her. "No," she said. "I just crossed the street."

It was a codifying moment for me, one of those small incidents in a long life that precisely exemplifies the person. This was Norma Anderson—private, calm, deliberate, strong, and courageous, making her way in the face of adversity that would have sent most of us running home.

Her husband, Dr. William G. Anderson, author of this book, is yang to her yin. Bill is impulsive, impetuous, constantly on the move, energizing those around him. He's most alive in public settings and maneuvers through a crowd, shaking hands like a square dancer

William G Anderson, DO, FACOS

doing a right and left grand. He's a consummate and inspirational public speaker, and his humor and empathy are magnetic.

As different as they were, they shared much: a common locus in history, passion for justice, love for humanity, extraordinary integrity, bottomless capacity for work, and intelligence. Most importantly, they shared the strength to listen to the small, still voices that have led them to respond in faith to make decisions that in foresight seemed risky and, in hindsight, proved keystones to success. In short, Bill and Norma Anderson broke through the glass ceiling of prejudice by stepping out on the glass floor of faith.

They were the foci of the Albany Movement, a civil rights effort seminal in changing the role of Blacks in American history. They befriended giants, including Martin Luther King Jr. and Ralph David Abernathy. Together, they reached a pinnacle of the osteopathic profession—family physician, board-certified surgeon, prominent medical educator, hospital administrator, and president of the national American Osteopathic Association. They raised highly successful children and have numerous grandchildren and great-grandchildren. They have loved, laughed, wept, traveled, played, argued, challenged, won, and lost. Theirs are lives well lived.

This project has been a great privilege for me. I marched as a college student for civil rights in the 1960s. I have stood at the Atlantic Ocean's eastern shore at Ouidah, Benin, where millions of slaves were exported, and at its western shore at Charleston, South Carolina, and Savannah, Georgia, where they were imported. To be a close witness to the graceful and successful lives of these grandchildren of American slaves is somehow balm to wounds of this horrific portion of our history, a testimony to all of us that even greed, murder, and torture cannot conquer the human spirit.

PAT GRAUER

Foreword
by Norma Anderson

IN 1957, AFTER MY HUSBAND completed his osteopathic medical internship in Flint, Michigan, we did not have much money. Andy (as he was called) was paid $50 per month, his stipend as an intern at Flint Osteopathic Hospital. I had a job with the Flint public school system and taught at Roosevelt Elementary School. The year of his internship went by swiftly. We had several offers after Andy completed his internship, and I had been offered a scholarship by a civic club in Flint to continue my education at the University of Michigan.

During the first week of June 1957, most schools were preparing to close for the summer. Teachers were busy with tests, programs, picnics, and other activities. Many children were joyous and excited, but others were solemn and sad about having to leave friends and teachers. There was much anticipation of what they were going to do that summer.

In addition to all the school activities and taking care of my family, I was five months pregnant, and I still had to complete year-end report cards for the students. This was a trying experience. I had taught semi-platoon classes—the fourth, fifth, and sixth grades in arts and science in the mornings and kindergarten in the afternoon.

Andy was in his last week of the internship, and this was also the time designated for graduation ceremonies for interns and residents.

Earlier in May, Andy took the children and me for a ride to show us houses—each a two-story complex—where we could live, and he could open an office downstairs. He had already made up his mind to stay in Flint. Somehow, I kept remembering our plans from an earlier time. I was not saying anything, and he finally said, "You are not happy, and I'd like to know why."

All that week, I had the most peculiar feeling, but it was not connected with my physical condition. I could not understand my uneasiness. I certainly had no wish to start an argument. After thinking for a while, I said, "We cannot stay in Flint, Andy. Remember, we said we'd go back to the South and help our people after you finished your training."

He was quiet and said nothing else. Andy did not take what I had said seriously. He was not going to leave Flint. One day, Andy called from the hospital and said, "Norma, we're going to visit Bud and Ginger this afternoon."

I told my sister Juanita, who was also a teacher and was living with us, about the conversation. She was a great help to the family, as she shared the household expenses and helped me with cooking and caring for the children. This was her week to cook, and she was cooking at the time of our conversation. She said, "Go on, I'll take care of the children."

Bud Edwards was a reading psychologist for Flint Public Schools and an instructor at the University of Michigan. Andy and I did not have much time to socialize, but we did keep in touch with Bud and Ginger.

Ginger would bring her children over to our home to visit me and our children. On many Saturdays, we would have brunch that Ginger cooked. Ginger was an intelligent woman whose opinion on many subjects her husband respected.

Foreword

Bud and Ginger were expecting us. When Andy and I arrived at their home, we were escorted into the living room, where we were offered hors d'oeuvres and drinks.

Ginger started the conversation, "Norma, why do you want to leave Flint and go south? We love you and Andy. He'll have a lucrative practice in Flint, and you have a good job teaching. This is a good school system for the children. You have many friends at Mt. Olive Baptist Church. Other people are also concerned about your leaving."

I thanked them for their concern, care, and friendship and replied, "A long time ago, Andy and I talked about going back to a small town in Georgia. We could help so many people in need of good medical care. At this time, so many Black people in the South have inadequate health care. Black people who go to White doctors have to wait in a back room, often a closed-in back porch. Many Negroes are treated like cattle in the basement of a hospital, or in an undesirable wing of the hospital, if they provide space for Negro patients at all. We will try to change some of that."

Andy was quiet the whole time. I cannot remember all that I said, but I talked about the plight of Black people. So many young people, as well as many adults, had low self-esteem because of the way they were treated. At this time in history, so many Black people were unhappy. The problem was not only in the South; it was all over the United States. It was just more apparent in the South, and we could make a difference.

Finally, Bud responded, "Excuse me, Norma. Andy, go home and pack your things." After compassionate goodbyes, we left.

It was hard leaving our friends in Flint. We would miss people at Mt. Olive Baptist Church, Flint Osteopathic Hospital, and the teachers and students at Roosevelt Community School.

It was particularly hard for me to leave my sister, who had no other relatives in Flint. Juanita assured me that everything would be all right. As a family, we got through this phase in our lives, and the children were fairly content with leaving.

At Andy's graduation banquet for interns and residents in June

1957, the speaker ended with a story: "I would like to tell you a story of a young doctor who went to a small town to practice. He became well-known in the community. He was not only the town's doctor but also a friend and counselor to the people. He practiced medicine until he was an old man. When he died, the townspeople mourned his death and wondered what they could do to commemorate his passing. One man suggested putting his office sign on his tombstone, which they did. His office was on the second floor of a building, and his sign simply read: 'DR. UPSTAIRS.'"

The story reaffirmed our commitment to return to the South. We knew there would be places in Georgia where we could not enter. There would be signs on restroom doors that said "COLORED." On buses, the signs would say, "WHITES UP FRONT, BLACKS TO THE BACK." We knew we could not eat in White-owned restaurants or stay in White hotels or motels. We had both gone to segregated schools in Georgia, but we also remembered teachers who loved children and cared about the future. We remembered how old books from White schools were handed down to us in Black schools, while White students got new editions. Yes, Jim Crow was alive and well in the South. We also knew these attitudes would continue to thrive unless Black people made a concerted effort to improve their lot. We had to do our part. This was time to begin my walk and for Andy to help change the course of history.

NORMA ANDERSON

Foreword

...to read Norma Anderson's memoirs, see her book *The Moving Walkway*.

Contents

About this Book	1
Foreword *by Pat Grauer*	3
Foreword *by Norma Anderson*	5
Author's Note	13
Growing Up in Americus, Georgia	19
Big Man on Campus	29
Navy Man	33
Beginning Again After The War	45
Montgomery Mortician	53
The Return to Atlanta	57
Transforming into an Osteopathic Physician	67
An Osteopathic Intern in Michigan	81
A Physician in Albany	87
A Member of the Albany Community	99
The Albany Movement	109
The Battle Is Joined	123
The Move Back North	159
The Making of a Felon	165
Civil Rights in Detroit	171
Freedom Redefined	177
Growing as a Surgeon and a Leader	183
Hospital Administration and Education	195
Climbing the Ladder in the Osteopathic Profession	201
A Rolling Stone	209
The Challenge of Golf	215
My Religion	223
All Our Children	229
A Brush with Death	241
From Slavery to Freedom: An American Odyssey	247
In Closing	261
Vignettes	267
Special Recognition Awards	271
Thank You For Reading My Book!	275

Author's Note

In your hands you hold my life story, a story I delayed putting into words because I felt that I was immortal and would be here forever. I could not imagine a time when I would no longer be able to enjoy the benefits of being alive: the pleasures of recreation (especially golf), the joy of having a large family, the extraordinary love that has been demonstrated by my grandchildren to me and the tremendous satisfaction that I have received from the successes of my children. I reflect with considerable pride on the fact that my marriage survived for well over a half-century—a marriage that started in an unconventional manner in that we both were college students. There was no long courtship, no formal proposal, and no father of my fiancée to ask for her hand. That it lasted so long, I can only attribute to the love, devotion, commitment, and faith of a wife who was willing to see beyond my faults and find something of value in me—even in those times when I could not see it.

I dedicate this book to my beloved Norma, who has preceded me to her resting place; my children and my grandchildren, for through all of the experiences I have had, these are the ones who have made my life worth living; and to the American Osteopathic Foundation, who will receive all proceeds from this book to further endow a scholarship program established by Norma and me more than 25 years ago.

My story is a braid of several notable lives I have led, including radio entertainer, educator, mortician, a seaman in the U.S. Navy, physician, and Civil Rights Movement activist. Being a physician seems to be somewhat incompatible with being a mortician, but that contradiction, and others, is part of what has made me who I am.

My most important roles, as a civil rights activist and as an osteopathic physician, I did not choose; it was as if fate had thrust them upon me, determined by factors that even I find difficult to explain. Both were influenced directly by my choice of a wife, and both thrust me unexpectedly into national roles of leadership. I did not foresee that I would lead the seminal Albany Movement in Georgia, and that my wife's childhood neighbor, Martin Luther King Jr., and my college classmate, Ralph David Abernathy, would join forces to change the face of America. I did not foresee when I applied to osteopathic medical school that I would rise to the highest pinnacle of that profession to become the president of its national organization, the American Osteopathic Association (AOA).

Even my service in the United States Navy near the end of World War II was a study in contradictions. I volunteered because I felt it was the right thing to do. I was a patriot wanting to serve in the defense of my nation, which I felt had been unjustly and unfairly attacked by the Japanese. I felt an obligation and responsibility to protect my family and my country, notwithstanding the fact that I had grown up in a totally segregated society, at best treated as a second-class citizen, and at worse, operated as an indentured servant with limited liberties that only Whites enjoyed.

Caution to Readers

It is only fair that readers of this autobiography are cautioned about my mental status and mindset. It may serve to know that I have bouts

Author's Note

of paranoia and multiple personality disorder. These are not unusual traits for an African American who grew up in the 20th century and was a little more than a generation removed from slavery.

My paranoia stems from my experiences growing up in a racist society. Whenever there seemed to be some improvement in race relations or I was beginning to enjoy life, liberty and the pursuit of happiness, there would be an event or organized group determined to turn back progress. Following the abolition of legal institutionalized and commercialized slavery, there was an era of shadow slavery. This era was perpetuated by the likes of the Ku Klux Klan, White Citizens Council, skinheads, Nazis, Aryans, some militiamen, and perhaps some well-meaning and good-intentioned Whites who did nothing to counteract the effects of racism. There was an adequate reason for my paranoia, and occasionally, it has served me well in keeping my defenses up to avoid reverting to a slave mentality.

My multiple personalities were, in part, caused by the numerous identities that I acquired during my lifespan. I was born colored. It is so indicated on my birth certificate. There were those who could not quite pronounce "colored," and it sounded more like "cullud." Then I became Negro, which was the most widely accepted identity by those of us of color as well as some of the more charitable Whites. There were those who had difficulty pronouncing "Negro," and it came out "Negra," and of course, there were those not-so-charitable people who referred to us as "niggers." Needless to say, this designation of my racial identity was as objectionable then as it is today.

It was many years before I became Black. This is not to say that I did not know that I was part of the Black race, but that "Black" carried a negative connotation and, therefore, was found to be objectionable. It was not until the era of H. Rap Brown and Stokely Carmichael that we began to accept our blackness and wore the identity with great pride. "I'm Black, and I'm proud" became a rallying call for many of us early in the Civil Rights Movement.

Later, I came to accept the identity of Afro-American. This was the first attempt to link the Blacks in America to our African ancestry.

William G Anderson, DO, FACOS

While few of us could directly trace our roots back to Africa, we readily accepted the linkage, for there was no historical evidence of any other heritage. The acceptance of this identity was enhanced by Alex Haley with his award-winning book and television series entitled *Roots*.

It was a matter of evolution as we moved from Afro-American to African American. I believe this was an attempt to be consistent with the identities of others who had migrated from other countries to America. There were the British American, French American, Italian American, Polish American, and others who assumed an identity that linked them with their past. This was especially important as those of European descent brought with them cultures, religions, customs, and traditions that were preserved in the new society, while Black African slaves were robbed of their identity, heritage, culture, religion, and customs.

It is an important distinction between those who came to America and those who were brought to America. Most Europeans came to America voluntarily, seeking a better way of life. African slaves were brought to America against their will, in bondage, and were sold, bartered, and traded as chattel or cattle. It is unfair to compare those who came to America with those who were brought to America and then to expect the same final American product.

While it is impossible to trace my roots directly back to Africa, I have no difficulty in identifying with the plight of the African slaves who were brought to this country. I appreciate the fact that the opportunities of my life emerged because these slaves overcame overwhelming obstacles. For them, there were three major imperatives. First, of course, was survival. It is estimated that more than 10 million Blacks did not survive the passage of the slave trade. Chained and forced to live in the stinking, crowded, and dark hulls of ships, slaves were transported in the most inhumane conditions that one can possibly conceive. Health care was nonexistent, nutrition was wholly inadequate, and the lives of the slaves were expendable. Their value was only determined by their worth at the marketplace. Mere

Author's Note

survival depended on the mental, physical, and emotional capabilities of the slaves.

Second, they had to establish a positive identity as humans. Slaves were regarded as the same as cattle, and their perceived value was their ability to provide an easier and better life for their slave masters. Slaves were stripped of their identity for centuries, only to be provided one by Whites following the Emancipation Proclamation. It is understandable that I would go from colored to Negro to Black to Afro-American and finally to African American. I was trying vainly to find an identity that was unique and one that would reflect and portray my ancestry.

The third imperative was that of transforming a racist nation, built on exploitation, into a free and open society with liberty and justice for all. This is a continuing imperative, even well into the 21st century. Three hundred years of literal slavery and 100 years of virtual slavery have both managed to survive the Constitution, the Bill of Rights, the Emancipation Proclamation, civil rights legislation, and hundreds of bits of legislation designed to put an end to segregation and discrimination. There is no due date for racism. We have found that universal freedom and justice are yet elusive and can never be considered a destination, but instead a continuing journey.

Lest I forget, I should also warn you that I am also a convicted felon. While fully pardoned some 50 years after the fact, the sentence stayed with me for more than half my life. My involvement with Martin Luther King Jr. and Ralph David Abernathy earned me this dubious distinction. It is a badge I have worn proudly, as have many others who participated in the Civil Rights Movements of the 1950s and 1960s.

Growing Up in Americus, Georgia
1924–1939

Americus was a small, rural town in southwest Georgia, which, like other communities in the South, was totally segregated. This was primarily a farming town, with a cotton gin and a pecan factory as the principal industries. To a lesser extent, there were peanuts, potatoes, and peaches. Segregation and discrimination could be defined by what was found in Americus. Our school systems were totally segregated, although never having lived in an integrated community, this did not appear to be out of the ordinary to us. We did notice that we always managed to get second-hand textbooks, full of inaccurate and outdated information, first used and discarded by White students.

I grew up in a community where at no time was there any mixing of the races in education, in social or civic life, no personal or cordial relationship between Blacks and Whites. Their only relationship was transactional: that of employer-employee or merchant-customer. There was no such thing as a Black policeman or fireman or public official. Blacks did not register to vote or hold public office, nor did they complain about it. We were told, "Voting is White folks' business, and ain't nothing for you colored folks to be concerned about."

In this context, we were considered an ordinary, or perhaps above ordinary, Black family for a small, rural town in Georgia. Ironically, the highest compliment ever paid to the Anderson family was, "They raised their children like White children." We were quite proud when a White neighbor made that statement, as we had been conditioned to believe that standards set by White people were the ones to be emulated. But it was in that same society where my father and mother never became "Mr." and "Mrs." My father went from "Boy" to "Uncle," and my mother went from "Girl" to "Auntie" or "Annie." Later, after the Civil Rights Movement of the 1960s, I had risen to the top in the osteopathic profession, and I was installed as president of the American Osteopathic Association. At my inauguration, I proclaimed, "I am happy to announce that my mother has lived long enough to become Mrs. Anderson in Georgia." This was one of my proudest moments.

A Mischievous Youth

My family was considered upper class in Americus in that both of my parents had completed high school and my father some college by the time I was born. It was not until some years later that my mother enrolled in college to pursue her degree in education. She had already become employed by the school system with a high school diploma, which placed her in an education class above the majority of the "coloreds" in town. My father, with some college education, was the district manager of the North Carolina Mutual Life Insurance Company, one of the few Black-owned insurance companies in America.

Much of my youth was spent in school and church activities, as there were very limited social outlets otherwise. I also had the experience of doing some farm work at a young age. It was not a bit unusual to have a small farm at home, and we raised corn and greens and sweet potatoes and beans. We also had a few pecan trees, a mulberry tree, and a grapevine.

Growing Up in Americus, Georgia

In my early school years, the high point of recreation was slipping off to the swimming hole. In reality, it was nothing more than a large drainage ditch that collected water from the streets following a rainfall, and from other sources like garages and the factories. There was never any consideration as to what kinds of pollutants were in the swimming hole, and to our knowledge, no one ever got sick from swimming there. The alternative for swimming in the drainage ditch was in the local creek, a small stream that flowed around the outskirts of Americus. It was muddy and lined by poisonous snakes that did not at any time deter us from

swimming. We were not aware of any of my playmates getting bitten by snakes while swimming in this creek, and all felt as though a water moccasin could not bite underwater or he would drown. As an adult, it never ceases to amaze me how ignorance served as a protective barrier against such potential harm.

There was one theater in town, the Rylander. Growing up, there was a "colored" entrance and a "White" entrance. The colored people could sit in the third balcony most of the time, and occasionally were allowed to sit in the second balcony when there was a movie that featured Black entertainers. It was always a treat to go to the movies, where I managed to spend most Saturday evenings. I thought nothing of sitting in the balcony, which we referred to as the Buzzards' Roost. I would go to the movies in the early afternoon on Saturday and stay until late Saturday night—first out of interest in the double features, with usually a comedy and the news. But I also stayed out of concern for my safety in going from the theater to my home, which was a distance of only three short blocks.

Somehow, one of my schoolmates was always aware of when I would be leaving the movies and would lie in wait for me in one of the dark, unlighted streets and chase me home. I can only imagine that his attacks on me were provoked by jealousy in that my parents appeared to have more than the average of the coloreds in Americus. It was many years later that I learned that both my sister and brother had been subjected to the same kind of harassment by the same student. I often wonder what happened to this menace but never tried to find out. I suppose that it was the kind of experience that many had growing up in a community with the "haves" and the "have-nots." My family—with educated, employed parents, a home, car, and a small bank account—placed us in that category of the "haves," and that made us the envy of some.

Schooling

I started school at a very young age. There was no nursery or kindergarten to attend, so when children were old enough to count to 10 and recite the ABCs and were out of diapers, they were permitted to start the first grade. Somehow, I managed to graduate from high school at the tender age of 15.

My elementary and high school teachers were exceptional in that they took a personal interest in me. This was evident in the numerous episodes of corporal punishment, which was permitted in the schools as I was going up. Though I was frequently an unwilling participant in these rituals, I must admit that I was most deserving.

Miss Eliza Bethune was my sixth-grade teacher. She took a particular interest in me, not so much for my scholarly activities as in my companionship. I was quite talkative and good company to be around. Miss Bethune, as was the case for many elementary and high school teachers, was an old maid. "Old maid" was not considered derogatory; however, one never referred to unmarried teachers in their presence as "old maids."

Miss Bethune, who enjoyed jaunts all over the United States and Canada, desired a traveling companion and selected me. I was quite honored to be so selected, and enjoyed the travels as it afforded me the opportunity to gain experiences that I could not have imagined otherwise. I remember vividly trips to Niagara Falls, Chicago, and Radio City Music Hall in New York. It was on one of the trips to New York that I first saw television in its infancy. It was on a tiny, six-inch screen in a huge box and was only telecast from one studio to the other.

It was also with Miss Bethune that I had the opportunity to attend the World's Fair in Chicago. To me, these travels were fun, though I did not fully appreciate them until much later in life.

I was quite mischievous as a young boy growing up in Americus. Never anything vicious or malicious—just mischievous. Frequently I would get into small scrapes and would often get beaten because my fighting skills were somewhat lacking. Yet I was quite popular in high school. Having a girlfriend was the furthest thing from my mind because I thought that girls were absolute nuisances, so my social interaction was limited to official school functions. I was not very good at athletics, and though I tried out for the basketball and football teams, I found my niche on the cheerleading squad. The highest compliment ever paid to me by the football coach (who was also my shop instructor) was, "I have always known Anderson to have a big mouth, and he will make a good cheerleader." However, my cheerleading career was not very exciting in that my high school football team won very few games.

I was always in the shadow of my older brother (JD), who was a very good student and a talented musician. He played the piano and violin, both of which I detested. Each of us Anderson children was given the opportunity to study music, but I consistently resisted it. In frustration, my mother gave me a choice of studying piano or selling newspapers. I chose selling newspapers, and for several years peddled the Atlanta Daily World. I failed miserably, for I frequently missed sales or failed to collect or ate up all of the profits. Unfortunately, there was a concession stand on my paper route that seemingly absorbed all of my potential profits.

So, I finished high school with no money from the sale of newspapers, no musical abilities because I declined to take lessons, and no scholarships, for I barely did well enough to get a diploma. I managed by some mystery to graduate from high school and was duly recognized by the principal, E.J. Grandberry, as the one least likely to succeed in anything. Three high school principals came and left during my four years at A.S. Staley High. I cannot say that I was the cause of their leaving, but none of them would say that they were not happy to show me their backs. They had not heard of "no child left behind," or they would not have been so eager to leave me behind. Such was my life in Americus, Georgia.

My Family

My older brother (JD), younger sister (Dorothy Jean, but goes by Jean), and I grew up in a loving family, one in which we early on came to appreciate the value of both education and hard work.

My father was quite short, measuring only about 5 feet 5 inches, and he had a light complexion and very thin, straight black hair. He was small in stature but a giant of a man in the eyes of those who knew him. He was always cheerful and full of life. His career as an insurance salesman fit him like a glove, because he loved people, and they, in turn, loved him. As young children, my brother, sister, and I enjoyed trav-

eling around in south Georgia with Dad as he collected insurance premiums. Often, his clients did not have the money and paid him with farm products such as butter, eggs, and syrup. Occasionally, there would be a country salt-cured ham shoulder or butt that made the trip worthwhile. It did not seem to matter that we would occasionally have to stop to repair a flat tire. Tubeless tires had not yet been invented, and we had to learn how to repair an inner tube with glue and a rubber patch. We loved our dad for many reasons, but these little experiences made us feel both wanted and needed.

As district manager of the North Carolina Mutual Insurance

Growing Up in Americus, Georgia

Company, my father had an office and a staff of agents and secretaries. I would delight in going to his office to play with the upright Underwood typewriter and the National adding machine. I learned to type by watching my father at the Underwood keys, where he could bang out a letter at the rate of 90 words a minute with a comparable number of errors. But who cared? He got the job done, and he was impressive with his two-finger speed. I learned to type the same way and still use two fingers, but I can more easily correct my errors thanks to the computer and Microsoft Word.

My father had attended Morehouse College, one of the most prestigious colleges for Black males in the United States. There was some question as to whether he ever received a degree, but that was not important because he was considered a "Morehouse Man" simply because he attended. We all took great pride in the fact that our father was one of the few men from Americus who ever made it to college.

My mother was a schoolteacher with only a high school education from Americus Institute, a private boarding school. Her limited education far exceeded that of most in our community and much of the rural South. She later received a degree by going to college in the summer and working as a teacher during the winter, while making what would be considered a far below poverty-level salary.

Being inspired and encouraged and supported by these loving parents, the three of us—my brother, my sister, and I—all received college degrees and were given every opportunity for advanced study, notwithstanding the meager means of our parents. It was my mother who said to me when I had been accepted into osteopathic medical school with no idea how I could possibly afford it, "Go on, William. Do it. We'll find a way." That was all I needed to hear: "Just go on and do it. We'll find a way."

My family hated but tolerated the conditions of segregation and discrimination, feeling as though they had no choice but to do what was necessary to survive in a racist society. There were major voids in my family tree, the reasons for which were not apparent at the time.

William G Anderson, DO, FACOS

As I grew older, I began to understand and appreciate the fact that some Blacks who were direct descendants of slaves were ashamed to speak of the conditions under which their parents and grandparents had existed as slaves. We came to realize that this was in part because many liberties were taken by the slave masters with the female slaves, and the males were treated harshly or subjected to lynching for what were considered indiscretions in their relationships with Whites, especially White women.

So, little was spoken of my ancestors. It was only in later years that I attempted, with the aid of my sister, to reconstruct a family tree, only to find that documentation was lacking. We went so far as to retain the services of a professional genealogist to discover our roots. She tried unsuccessfully and returned our deposit, stating that my sister had gone as far as anyone could possibly go in searching out our family history. We had to settle for what we could find on the grave markings and in the county courthouse records.

What little we know of my mother's parents was that they died when she was a pre-teen, and no one ever spoke of them until much later. My mother did have a brother and a sister and several aunts and uncles, and we, in fact, acted as a family with traditional family reunions in Moultrie, Georgia. "It takes a village" took on real meaning in my mother's family.

Aunt Ethel Finney, whom we children thought was one of the meanest people in the world, was a strict disciplinarian. It's not as though we did not need to be disciplined, but like all sub-teens and teenagers, we rebelled against the rules imposed by our elders. Aunt Ethel and Uncle Finney were wonderful, caring relatives who willingly took in our mother when she was orphaned and eventually cared for my mother's children as if they were their own. They never had biological children, so I, along with my brother, JD, and sister, Jean, became their grands.

Aunt Ethel and Uncle Finney were part of the Lee family, that was well-known in southwest Georgia. The senior Lee brothers were very industrious. Uncle Johnny was a successful businessman and owned

Growing Up in Americus, Georgia

a funeral home, a farm and a lot of real estate. As a young, eager teenager, I looked forward to the opportunity of working on his farm, picking cotton and stacking tobacco. It was especially fun to sell watermelons that were left over from the market. All of the remaining watermelons were dumped on Aunt Ethel's front lawn, where we would sell them: all you can carry for five cents.

Uncle Joe Lee, with his secret sauce, was the barbecue king of southwest Georgia. His reputation was known for miles around, and he made a comfortable living selling barbecue and Brunswick stew (also from a secret recipe). He also had a reputation for frequent marriages. It was always an exciting experience to visit with him, first for the barbecue but even more so to get to meet the current Mrs. Joe Lee. We were never sure that Uncle Joe had bothered to divorce one before marrying another, but we also were not sure that he had ever married any of them.

Uncle Doty Lee was the contractor and builder in the family, well-known and respected for his skills as a brick mason and carpenter. Uncle Doty constructed many buildings in and around Moultrie. He trained many of the male members of the family to become accomplished builders. Uncle Doty was fond of goldfish and dogs, both of which he had at all times.

Uncle Tommy Lee, who had lived in New York, returned to Moultrie after the untimely death of Uncle Johnny to take over his businesses. Ironically, Uncle Johnny, who had owned the funeral home, was killed in a tornado while picking up a dead body from the train station.

There were many other relatives in Moultrie who made it the home for the Lee family and all of its descendants. The Bradberrys and Youngs—all prominent citizens of Moultrie who became teachers, builders, and leaders in business—were all part of the extended Lee family.

My father had a sister and a mother, but we were not aware of any other close relatives. There were scarcely any discussions about his father, and never can I remember any reference being made about his grandparents. My paternal grandfather was thought to have been Native American. This impression was enforced by the single photograph that we had of him: his complexion was light, and he had long, straight, coal-black hair.

My paternal grandmother, whom we called Big Mama, was a tough disciplinarian. The three of us, JD, Jean, and I, spent many summers with Big Mama in Cordele, Georgia. I cannot say that they were very pleasant summers, but they were memorable. It was hard to forget the outhouse at the end of the alley or the water well or the kerosene lamps used for lighting. Watching the "honey wagon" making its regular runs through the neighborhood was a revelation. Having an indoor toilet and running water had spoiled us.

My sister, Dorothy Jean, received a B.A. from the prestigious Talladega College in Alabama. After a short stint as a teacher, she pursued a career in social work and later in the field of telecommunications, retiring from AT&T. A marriage produced a daughter, Rhonda Jean, who graduated from the prestigious Spelman College with a degree in physics. After six years with Rockwell International working on parts for the space program, she followed her mother in the field of telecommunications. Though my brother followed in my father's footsteps and attended Morehouse College, I was more interested in going to college with my high school friends and classmates at a smaller college in the middle of Georgia, then known as Fort Valley State College.

Big Man on Campus
1939-1943

Poor high school grades, lack of athletic ability, no musical talents, discipline problems—all were handicaps that I carried from high school. Nonetheless, I managed to get accepted at Fort Valley State, a small college in the heart of Georgia with a reputation known only to people living within 100 miles of the town of Fort Valley. It was best known for its agriculture program, producing farmers, and for training teachers for home economics, but it was a fun place to be.

Fort Valley, like many other colleges, was feeling the impact of World War II as most of the male students had been drafted for the military. There was a total enrollment of 300, but to my dismay, only 26 of these were boys.

What a daunting task, I thought: *26 boys and 274 girls*. I faced the challenge with courage and determination. We had the patriotic duty to keep the home fires burning, to make certain that the girls left behind would not suffer from lack of male companionship. It was very difficult to visit three girls' dormitories in a single night with the severe time limitations and then to preserve the privacy and confidentiality essential in such relationships. It was even more difficult the day after the scheduled visitations to explain what happened the night before.

Fort Valley State College was not all fun and games. I enrolled in a pre-med curriculum with no thought of how I would ever gain admission to a medical school. Only one graduate of Fort Valley had ever achieved this goal, and he was a superior scholar. I was not a stellar student, yet I never failed a class. I was particularly good in the biological and chemical sciences. Western world literature and basket weaving were not my idea of preparing to become a doctor.

I began at Fort Valley at 15, the tender age of my graduation from high school. This was not too unremarkable in that there were no strict criteria for entering public school in Americus. I was out of diapers and able to understand some counting and some of the alphabet so I could enroll in the first grade. There was no preschool or kindergarten, and high school only went to the 11th grade. So, it is understandable that I could start first grade at the age of five (my birthday was in December, so I was old enough to get in under the wire). By the time I was 15, I had already finished the 11th grade and was eligible to attend college.

My parents, having very meager means and children who desired to go to college, could not provide the luxuries afforded by some of my classmates. However, my parents did manage to send me $25 a month, which took care of the necessities of room, board, and tuition. Extra money I earned working as a clerk in the campus snack shop and as an assistant mail carrier to my very close friend Rochelle Harris. I guess you could call it doing what was necessary to survive, but I only considered it a part of getting an education coming from a family stretched financially thin.

While at Fort Valley, I had the good fortune of meeting and working for one of the premier Black educators and authors in the nation, Horace Mann Bond, president of Fort Valley State College. He picked me to be his personal chauffeur, as he traveled extensively through Alabama and Mississippi writing about the educational system for Blacks in those Southern states. He had a tremendous influence on my life and my desire to advance my education. Once, he said to me, "What a checkerboard life you have lived!" Even though I was a college student with limited experience, the statement was both descriptive and prophetic. In the short years that I had been living, I had worked as a bellhop, a bartender, a laborer, and a farmhand, and yet often spoke of one day becoming a physician and surgeon.

I was later introduced to Hermes Johnson, an instructor in French, who also selected me as her personal chauffeur. I was given the opportunity to travel extensively with her throughout the Southern states. She, too, had an influence on my subsequent educational career.

The most influential of all of my professors during my early college years was William Boyd, a sociologist who took a keen interest in his students and would informally engage them in conversation about their plans, their ambitions, and their futures. On one such occasion I told him I was becoming disenchanted with a college education and thought seriously about quitting in my second year. It was William Boyd who said, "If you quit now, what will you be able to do that millions of others cannot do?" That was enough motivation for me not to stop, but rather to continue with my education.

Looking back on my years at Fort Valley State College, I realize that this small Georgia college had more to offer in the development of men and women than most colleges of its size. Fort Valley State had a system called the "Scope Chart," designed to evaluate the total development of students. The chart included culture, custom, attitude, integrity, self-esteem, pride, confidence, and self-respect—character traits that were considered as important as academics. No other college, to my knowledge, had such a system. To many students this was a painful burden, but it proved to be of enormous benefit to produce well-rounded, well-adjusted, capable, competent, reliable, responsible adults.

Fort Valley State will be best remembered as the place where I met the one who would be my first true love, the mother of my children, and my companion through the good, the bad, and the ugly—and I gave her all of them. God has never made a more loving, compassionate, patient, forgiving, and insightful woman than the one who would become my wife. Without her, I would never have accomplished all that I have in this most remarkable life.

Were it not for my marriage to Norma Dixon, I would not have met and befriended Martin Luther King Jr. and Ralph David Abernathy. I would not have known William Holmes Borders, Roland Smith, and B.J. Johnson, who, along with Martin Luther King Sr,. were among the best-known preachers of this nation. Without Norma, I would not have been able to survive the rigors of medical school, would not have returned to Albany after becoming an osteopathic physician (D.O.), and would not have had the unique opportunity of becoming a part of the history of America in the Civil Rights Movement. I am eternally grateful to Norma for all I have become and expect to come. She also brought me great joy and pride in giving me five outstanding children, many grandchildren, and great-grandchildren, who give meaning and purpose to life and beyond.

Navy Man
1943–1945

During this time, World War II was well underway. The Germans under Adolf Hitler's regime were making their move toward conquering the world. The Japanese, who attacked Pearl Harbor unprovoked, augmented their efforts. This incensed the nation, and I can still remember the words of President Franklin D. Roosevelt that were printed in bold letters across the front page of the local newspaper, *The Times Recorder*, under the headline that read: "Japanese Attack Pearl Harbor." Roosevelt had said, "This is a day that will live in infamy."

Then, at my home on the radio, Roosevelt's words inspired a nation as well as me personally. I was motivated to join the military in defense of this country. I was too young for the draft and, as a matter of fact, too young to volunteer when World War II broke out, so I went on to college at the age of 15. By the time I was 16, many of my college classmates had gone off to war, and I was eager to join the military. Those who were not in the military were often questioned as to why. Every able-bodied, red-blooded American was in the military, or there must have been something horribly wrong with him.

I did not wait to be drafted. I did not want to have to explain to the girls why I was not in the military. I first attempted to volunteer for the Air Force at age 16, and because of my age, it required my parents' approval, which was denied by my mother. But when I reached 17, my mother felt there was no way she could keep me out any longer so she relented, and I volunteered for the U.S. Navy.

I could not perceive myself being a foot soldier, especially with my bad feet. I only made it into the Navy on the recommendation of a White, Southern physician at the induction center who came to my defense. He told the recruitment officer, "Flat feet don't bother dem culluds" because he knew one down in his hometown. "He could plow from sunup 'til sundown with feet flat as a pancake." I cannot remember thanking anyone more for a negative recommendation.

The vision that I had painted of men in the Army—soldiers under fire, crawling under barbed wire, and diving into foxholes—was not my idea of the way I wanted to fight this war. Being on a nice, clean ship and wearing a crisp, white uniform was more my kind of a fighter.

When I went to volunteer for the Navy, I was given an option of the branch of service that I would like to enter. I had no knowledge of there being more than one branch of the Navy, so I inquired as to what my options were. I was told that the first option was in the stewards' branch. I asked, "What is that?" I was told that the stewards cooked and cleaned the officer's cabins...

I stopped the recruiter at that point and said, "I don't care what the other branch is. It can be shoveling horse manure. I will take it. I do not want to join the Navy to be anyone's servant. I've done that all of my life."

The recruiter, with a smile, then directed me to the room for physical examination and I was scheduled to become a seaman.

I had little idea of the future that the Navy held for me, but I was most pleased that I would be given the privilege to serve my country, but of equal importance that I would not be in that class of the despised 4-Fs. These were those rejected for either physical or mental

Navy Man

defects or maladies that precluded their service in the military. None of my classmates and schoolmates wanted to be classified as "4-F."

Soon after my induction, I was sent to Camp Lawrence at the Great Lakes Training Camp just north of Chicago. There were about 100 of us in my company; all were Black, which was not unusual during World War II, for the military had not yet been integrated. Integration came sometime later during the administration of President Harry S. Truman. Little did we know that we had been selected as the first test company in history for integration into the Navy, though it did not escape our attention that all of the members of my company had a high school diploma, and most of us had some college education.

Soon after we began our training in Camp Lawrence, we were transferred to Camp Moffett, which, before our arrival, was an all-White battalion. Recognizing that we were the first to integrate a battalion, we were determined to prove our worth and show that we could be as good as, if not better than, any other sailors in the Navy. My company won every award on the drill fields, in the demonstration of manual skills, in communication, in artillery, and all of the aspects of our Naval training. We were proud of these accomplishments. I cannot say that we were responsible for the successful integration of the Navy, but it is clear had this not been a successful experiment, integration may have been further delayed.

I could not have predicted what the remainder of my Naval career would be like. As fate would have it, we all went home on "boot leave" after six weeks of intensive training, and we were expected to return after a two-week period for assignment to overseas duty. What happened next was one of those twists in my life that initially seemed a big disappointment and subsequently turned out to be to my ultimate benefit.

I developed a case of acute tonsillitis while on boot leave. I had a high fever and swollen tonsils that required the attention of a physician, who determined that it was not advisable to return to the Great Lakes at that time. The Navy granted me an extension of my leave, which resulted in my company being assigned overseas without me. Little did I realize at the time that all of my company had been assigned to the Seabees, the branch of the Navy primarily responsible for the construction of roads and bridges. It was most fortunate that I would miss that assignment, as that was among the last things that I wanted to do. I was given an independent assignment upon my return from boot leave, ultimately to be placed on a ship bound for the South Pacific.

I was initially sent from the Great Lakes Naval Training Center to Treasure Island in the Bay area of San Francisco. It was a long rail ride out to the West Coast and, for the most part, uneventful. The troop train was integrated as it left Chicago, and there was little evidence that racism would raise its ugly head. But these troops had not been prepared for the now-integrated Navy, and there were some White sailors with perceptions and attitudes that were a carry-over from the days of a segregated military.

It did not take long before the tranquil train ride turned into an unpleasant experience, as one of the White sailors, having consumed a more than adequate amount of beer, decided to start his own civil war. The conversation became quite loud as he shouted at a porter that he would "throw his Black ass off the train."

The porter, experienced in handling similar situations, replied, "I have been thrown off of better trains than this by better men than you." Enough said. The porter made his point, and we heard no more from the sailor.

Soon after, I was sent to Hawaii to receive my next assignment. It was thrilling to be on a Navy ship and to be sailing under the Golden Gate Bridge, one of the wonders of the world.

Not all on board were as thrilled as I was. Many of my shipmates were hanging over the rail before we got out from under the bridge, leaving behind the breakfast that they had eaten that morning and some, I suspect, even dinner from the day before. Seasickness for the first time became a reality, and those who experienced it both were afraid that they would die and were afraid that they would not. They

Navy Man

thought that death would be a pleasant relief, even at the hands of the Japanese, whom we would soon engage in battle.

Seaman William G. Anderson

For the 20 days and nights we were at sea, many did not leave the rail. Adjusting to the rocking motion of the ship was not an easy thing to do. I was among the fortunate few who never experienced the discomforts of seasickness. The same could not be said for my good friend Bob Russell. I met Bob when he was hanging over the rail, and he did not leave the spot that he had cordoned off for the entire trip from California to Hawaii.

The excitement of being on board a ship and sailing the Pacific was short-lived. Boredom set in rather insidiously. Those of us who were mere passengers and not a part of the ship's crew had no duty assignments and, therefore, had little to do. We busied ourselves with card games, reading, and plotting things that we would do onshore in Honolulu, most never to become real.

We were limited to saltwater showers only, and for those who have not tried to shower in saltwater, it is an experience without which you can live for a lifetime. The soap does not lather, and the body never feels clean after such showers. I could no longer tolerate myself, and therefore, in defiance of ship regulations, I took a freshwater shower, and it felt good. The refreshing feeling only lasted long enough for me to be reported to the Chief Boatswain's Mate, who promptly suspended all of my privileges and subjected me to disciplinary action in the form of hard manual labor in the hold of the ship. I became acquainted with the ship's boiler room, where I labored, painting, in multiple coats, with the standard Navy steel gray and in the sweltering heat of the boilers. One may ask, "Was a freshwater shower worth that?" At the time I thought so, but it was a feat not to be repeated.

Bob Russell came from Sullivan, Indiana, where he was a star football player. Sullivan is a small town in the south-central part of the state where there were few Blacks—too few for the town to make separate accommodations for the races. So, Bob grew up in a more or less sterile environment, sheltered from the racist practices of segregation. It helped that his complexion was also very fair, to the extent that in the shadows, he could pass for White, as did many fair-skinned Blacks.

Bob and I became close friends and stuck together throughout our stay in Pearl Harbor until we were shipped out to the Philippines. We explored the island of Oahu with all of its beauty and splendor. Honolulu was a Navy town where sailors were welcomed and treated well. This was understandable as Hawaii was yet recovering from the ravages of the vicious attack on Pearl Harbor. There were many remnants and reminders of that attack. The native Hawaiians felt as though we were their defenders and protectors. The beauty was not limited to the natural landscape and shorelines but extended well to the people of Hawaii, especially the women who were most gracious and eager to show their appreciation, sometimes in grass skirts, to those of us committed to protecting them. My stay in Hawaii was short, but the memories were long-lasting.

My assignment out of Pearl Harbor was on a destroyer escort destined for the Philippines Islands near the end of the war. The Japanese had officially surrendered, but the message had not yet reached many of the Japanese soldiers who had been left hidden in the jungles of the South Pacific. The major war activity had come to an end, and there were only sporadic outbreaks of battles. Ours could have been considered the mop-up fleet, as we rarely experienced any active fire as we entered the Philippines and sailed up to Subic Bay and finally down to the Leyte Gulf.

While en route, our ship came under fire by Japanese fighters who had not yet heard that the war was over. We did not suffer significant damage, and fortunately, we were not attacked by a kamikaze, the most feared of the Japanese fighters. Those of us who were not a part of the ship's company did not have battle stations and were locked in the sleeping quarters far below deck. I thought it was more frightening to be below deck, not knowing what was going on, than to be in the midst of the fight. So, immediately after the attack, I volunteered for duty and was assigned to an anti-aircraft gun. Much to my disappointment, I never got the opportunity to use my newly found skill beyond the practice drills. The remainder of the trip to the Philippine Islands was uneventful.

I had received an independent assignment not attached to a company for my overseas duty. A Naval medical officer sent out a questionnaire to all on board my ship to determine if any of us had any background in medicine, including pre-med students who had been either drafted or were volunteers. There was an acute shortage of hospital corpsmen in the South Pacific. While I had no idea how I would ever become a physician, I announced that I was a pre-med student and had taken courses consistent with a pre-med curriculum. I was thrilled to have been selected for training in the Philippines. So, my tour of duty with the Seventh Fleet was short-lived, for just as I was beginning to become acclimated as an assistant gunner on a destroyer escort, I was put on shore on Samar Island in the Leyte Gulf to attend Hospital Corpsman's School.

For six intensive weeks, I studied the naval textbook on medicine. I became a fully qualified hospital corpsman in six weeks, and I was assigned duties in a naval clinic and hospital. This was my first real taste of the practice of medicine. The duties were comparable to a primary care physician in that men in the Navy who became sick first saw a hospital corpsman who determined whether or not they needed to see a physician. I loved my training and enjoyed my remaining months in the Navy, caring for the sick and wounded Navy personnel.

It was on Calicoan, a small island east of the Leyte Gulf in the Philippines, where racism again raised its ugly head. Integration of the sailors was just beginning and many of the men yet stayed in segregated quarters. We all worked together and ate together, but there the association stopped. There were separate sleeping quarters and rarely did the White and Black Navy personnel socialize together. It was ironic that we had a common enemy yet had little in common among ourselves.

An incident in the chow hall, the nature of which was never revealed, precipitated a violent confrontation between a Black and a White serviceman. The incident escalated into a full-blown race riot, with the Blacks taking to the hills and the Whites taking to their quarters. There was sporadic gunfire exchanged between the Blacks and Whites, but there was no report of serious injury or death. The following morning, there was an apparent attempt to keep the races apart until peace could be re-established. Calm followed, and the races began to mix with a better understanding and tolerance of each other, or at least with an appreciation of the high cost of hatred.

There was heard the occasional reference to "gooks," the derogatory term used to describe the Filipinos. The "G" word was comparable to the "N" word used in reference to Blacks. Aside from this, there were no further racial episodes during my stay on the island.

Penicillin was in its infancy as the treatment for gonorrhea. Needless to say, there was much need for this drug among servicemen thousands of miles away from home. The dose was 10,000 units given in 10-cc doses every four hours for 24 hours. This, compared with 10 million units in a single dose in later practice, indicated a dramatic change in penicillin use.

I became very proficient at giving doses of penicillin. While I cannot say that I enjoyed giving injections, the techniques that I developed served me well in my later medical career.

All was not work on the islands. I made friends with many of the locals. One in particular was a physician trained at the University of Manila. I was given the opportunity to travel around the islands with him and observe him in practice. I never ceased to marvel at his medical knowledge and also his command of some 26 different

Navy Man

dialects in the Filipino language. He taught me as much of the language as he could during my tour. I took great pride in learning enough to communicate on a superficial level, and I believe there developed a mutual respect as I put forth the effort.

I felt comfortable going into the villages that were yet quite primitive. Many of the Filipinos lived in grass huts; the more affluent lived in tin or steel Quonset huts. I learned to enjoy many of their delicacies and even tolerated the rice wine that was very prevalent.

I was familiar with many of the creatures found in the wilds, as I was very adventurous as a child, but none of my experiences in Georgia prepared me for a confrontation with a giant python. One casual walk in the wilderness, coming eye to eye with a huge, ominous-looking creature, was sufficient evidence to convince me that this was not the place for me to be. Needless to say, I limited my exploration of the islands to the beaten paths thereafter.

As much as I had to do while in the Philippines, I often longed for home. I would frequently go to the coast and gaze across the waters toward the United States and wonder if I would ever get back to those I loved. I realized that it was too far to swim and too much water to drink, so I contented myself for a longer stay.

I have many pleasant memories of my stay on the Islands. Those memories come flooding back as I meet more and more Filipinos in Detroit. I had the opportunity to cement friendships that I perhaps would not have developed had I not experienced living in their native country. They usually are startled when I speak my few words of Tagalog, one of the many Philippine dialects. Someday, I would like to return for a visit as a civilian.

After about a year overseas, I was shipped back to the United States, where I was assigned shore duty on Treasure Island in the Pacific Bay between San Francisco and Oakland, California. There I stayed for the remainder of my naval career, assisting an old career Navy cook who had more hash marks than I had years of living. My discharge had been delayed because this chief needed an assistant, and the commanding officer of the base had merely sought out a

Black sailor to assist his "old friend," Chief Harry Burrows. Disappointed in not being discharged to go home, I did not realize that this was choice duty.

I made the most of my assignment as I became familiar with members of the ship's company. These were the most privileged of all enlisted men. My duties included checking in sailors returning from overseas and checking out those going home. Chores were completed by noon each day, and thus, I had the remainder of the day free. I could leave the base at any time and usually with two of the most precious commodities of the wartime era: steaks and butter. These got me invitations to many choice places where even money could not get you. It did not take me long to learn how to take full advantage of being in ship's company, and my disappointment turned into a celebration of my good fortune.

It was during one of my frequent visits to San Francisco that my youthful curiosity got the best of me, and I was tempted to try marijuana, commonly referred to as "grass." The most popular part of town in San Francisco was called the Fillmore District. Practically every person in the military who came through San Francisco visited this area. Servicemen and the few servicewomen who visited the Fillmore District were treated well and frequently invited to see and experience some of the more interesting attractions—those one could not necessarily find in the San Francisco Tourist Bureau guide.

I accepted such an invitation to try a "trip on the grass" that was readily available in the district. One trip was sufficient to convince me that I would never do it again. While "tripping," I was floating and found myself searching for parts of my body that seemed to have minds of their own. I found it difficult to even find my feet. After that experience I resolved to stick with soda pop and an occasional glass of wine, specifically, Dubonnet. Incidentally, at 15 cents a glass, that was the cheapest wine available in the bars of the district.

Needless to say, there were other "attractions" that I did not feel ready to experience, however tempting they may be. One of the reasons for caution was you never knew if the invitation that you

Navy Man

would accept was what you expected. Gender or gender orientation was always somewhat of a mystery. It is said that anything that you want, you can get in San Francisco, even when you were not certain what you were getting. This was especially true in the Fillmore District, and I soon learned that it was not an exaggeration. A visit to a famous nightclub called Pinocchio's erased all doubts about the uncertainties of San Francisco.

I stayed in San Francisco just long enough to get to like it a bit and begin to think, "Maybe I would like to live here." But then the time came for my discharge and return home to Americus and back to college. College led to marriage; marriage led to children; marriage and children held me together and motivated me to stay in school and to become a physician, fulfilling my life's ambition.

Beginning Again After The War
1946–1947

Upon my discharge from the Navy and return home, I made plans to return to Fort Valley State College to finish my studies in pre-med. I renewed my efforts to get into medical school by applying to every school that would give me a chance. My hopes were regularly and predictably dashed as all of the letters said essentially the same thing: *no*. Some had explanations; others did not bother to explain. My grades were not the best, my college was not accredited by any national agency, and I did not have a benefactor. Georgia medical schools were not considered by me or me by them because we both knew that no Black would ever get admitted. Most of the Northern medical schools limited their Black admissions to two percent, and that quota could be filled from their undergraduate schools.

My best hope for admission was to Meharry Medical College or Howard University, and even there, my chances were slim without a benefactor, outstanding grades, or a family tie. I almost resigned myself to the fact that I would never get into medical school and, therefore, should pursue a career in education. My hopes were revived when I met my wife-to-be, Norma Lee Dixon. It was like love at first sight. Her thoughts far outpaced mine as she had determined soon after we met that she would marry me. I did not stand a chance of escaping my future, for she had planned it for me. Nothing better could have happened to me at that stage in life. She not only became a stabilizing force but also was a continuous source of encouragement that would not let me give up on my dreams of becoming a doctor.

Our marriage after a short courtship in college took place in the office of the Justice of the Peace in Macon, Georgia, a short distance from Fort Valley. Our classmates and friends, Emmett Jones and Cornelia Robinson, stood with us. The honeymoon of necessity was delayed because I had a football game later that day, and besides, we had no money. Many honeymoons were promised for the future.

Norma and I left Fort Valley State College and moved to Atlanta, where we stayed with her family, and I enrolled in the Atlanta College of Mortuary Science. Norma's mother immediately became my other mother as she welcomed me into her home. Mother Mary Dixon was the kindest and gentlest woman I had ever met. She had the grace and charm of royalty. I could not help but admire and respect her. As a single divorced mom, she had raised and educated four children working as a secretary. She was multi-talented, as she also wrote editorials for a church newspaper and often researched and wrote theme papers for college and university students. *What a remarkable woman*, I thought! To buy a house, pay college tuition, and provide all of the love and attention that children want and need growing up was nothing short of miraculous. Mother Dixon deserved much more in life than she ever got. The husband who left her with four children and never provided for them did not dissuade her from being both a mother and a father. She was "Mother Dear" to all of the children, including our children and me. The grandchildren shortened it to just "Dear."

Her father, Norman Shepard, whom we all called "Granddaddy," the undisputed grand patriarch of the family, tried to help Mother Mary and her children. As hard as he tried, Mother Mary was determined to do it herself, and she did a remarkable job of it. She would often keep the checks that he would send her uncashed until the expiration date.

Grandmother Addie Shepard was the stabilizing force in the Shepard-Dixon family. She acquired the name "Sugar" from her grandchildren, and we were left with no other choice but to call her that, as she was not recognized by any other name. We do not know where the practice started and it was not important, for the grandchildren loved it and she enjoyed hearing it. She remained "Sugar" to all of us until her death at the age of 95. She was a remarkable woman and was capable of working miracles with very limited resources, especially in the kitchen. To say she was a great cook would be an understatement. Her cooking abilities exceeded description, and she did it in record time on a wood-burning stove. It was nothing short of amazing.

I delighted in testing "Sugar" on her culinary skills and would often challenge her to make homemade rolls and peach cobbler pie on a two-hour notice, as we were en route from Atlanta to Sylacauga, Alabama, where they lived. She never failed. To emphasize her skills, she would add a beef roast with carrots and potatoes. Needless to say, I always looked forward to visiting the Shepards' home.

Granddaddy Shepard was not the warm and fuzzy kind but was very well admired and respected as the head of the Shepard-Dixon family. Assuming the role of the authority figure for the family was easy for him, as he was trained by being pastor of a church and a leader in the community. He was a strong believer in the value of education and insisted that his grandchildren, me included, go as far as we could in school. He never stopped studying and became actively involved in the teaching of others. He supported the local schools of Sylacauga and joined the board of directors of Selma University in Alabama, which would later become one of the hotbeds of the Civil Rights Movement.

When I was at my lowest point during the heat of battle in the Albany Movement, deeply depressed, frustrated, and not knowing what to do, I turned to Granddaddy Shepard for consolation and renewed strength. Norma, in her usual calm and deliberate way, knew what I needed to continue to lead this most important event in our lives. It was Norma who spirited me away from a very stressful period of the demonstrations in Albany and took me to Tuskegee Veterans Hospital for my mental and physical health and to Granddaddy Shepard for my much-needed spiritual health. After a few days, I was able to return to continue the movement.

Grandaddy Shepard lived a long and fruitful life. He was pastor of the same church for more than forty-five years and was recognized by the town of Sylacauga, who named a street and a shopping center in his honor. He died in his mid-nineties after a seven-year protracted illness. His memory lingers on in the lives of those he touched, even more than a quarter of a century later.

Also among Norma's family was James, whom we called Big Brother; Charles, whom we called Little Brother; and a younger sister, whom we called "Pru." Her real name was Juanita, and no one could remember how she got the nickname of "Pru." We are not even certain of the spelling; we just said it, mimicking the pet name given to her by her Granddaddy Shepard.

Big Brother James was tall, well-spoken, and strikingly handsome with wavy brown hair—and he knew it. He had no problem attracting members of the opposite sex. His ambition in life was to become a preacher and perhaps a lover, and he was well qualified for both. Big Brother was a close friend of young Martin Luther King Jr., who lived across the street from Norma's childhood home. Not only were they schoolmates and running buddies, but they were aspiring preachers in the tradition of many in their families. Big Brother James admired and emulated his grandfather, Norman Shepard, a highly regarded pastor, religious leader, and respected educator. Reverend Shepard was admired as he had held many offices in the Baptist organizations of Alabama and in the National Baptist Convention. He was an outstanding gospel preacher who could inspire and motivate like none other I had heard. Granddaddy

Beginning Again After The War

Shepard was a spirited preacher who could whoop, moan and groan, holding his congregation spellbound. Few preachers possess those talents. James' idols were also the likes of Adam Clayton Powell, William Holmes Borders, Billy Sunday, and J. Raymond Henderson —all outstanding preachers.

Young Martin Luther King Jr. was just as motivated to become a great preacher like his father, grandfather, and uncle. Martin's father became "Daddy King" to all of us who knew him. To know him was to love him and he was always a source of inspiration. Daddy King was pastor of the historic Ebenezer Baptist Church, a landmark on Auburn Avenue, a few short blocks from downtown Atlanta. Big Brother and Martin would practice their preaching on me *ad infinitum* and *ad nauseam*. Little did I realize that I was being irritated and bored by one who would become a Nobel Prize winner and a leader of a major revolution in America that would impact generations to come.

Eventually, Big Brother and Martin became schoolmates at Morehouse College, one of the most prestigious Black all-male colleges in the nation. It was Morehouse that they came under the influence of Benjamin Mays, the college president and one of the most highly regarded educators in America. It was also at Morehouse that they got exposed to the best Black preachers in the country. Morehouse was a private school that did not have the same restrictions as the state-supported schools. Therefore, Morehouse could invite controversial Black scholars of the time. Morehouse College had long been established as a prime source for excellent preachers and other business and professional men. To graduate from the "House" was an automatic ticket to the job market, especially to churches looking for new preachers.

Big Brother was called to pastor a church in Alabama while still a student. Preaching was his calling and his passion, but time would later reveal his lack of preparation, stability, and maturity. Big Brother also had some wild oats to sow. His pastorate was short-lived, and he was drawn to other interests that included marriage and a stint in the

William G Anderson, DO, FACOS

Army. He came to visit Norma and me in an Army captain's uniform, and he introduced himself as a chaplain. I cannot say that we knew for certain that he had attained the rank of captain in such a short time, but he certainly did look and act the part, so we accepted it.

To have Big Brother James visit our home was always a memorable experience, full of surprises that may be better characterized as shocks. After the first few visits and the accompanying "surprises," we became shell-shocked. We knew whenever he visited, he would leave a trail. One that would be difficult at best to follow but one that would be costly and littered with broken hearts and disappointments. He could be very impressive and persuasive with everyone he met.

Big Brother never really found himself or the place where he was destined to be in this life. After several attempts to get back into the ministry and his failure to find happiness in marriage, he fell into poor health and suffered an untimely death. I could only think, "What a tremendous loss to the family, to the ministry, and to society." He had so much potential and could have been a great preacher.

Little Brother Charles was equally handsome with coal-black, wavy hair. He was not as polished as Brother James, but just as capable of attracting female company. There was a steady stream of beautiful girls visiting the Dixons' home. We were never sure of Little Brother's interest in pursuing a career, but he did continue in school and graduated from college. It was apparent that he had no interest in the ministry. His education was interrupted by a brief stint in the Army.

Charles was very open and friendly. It was hard for anyone not to like him. His ease of developing close friends resulted in his being in the proverbial "wrong place at the wrong time." He was visiting the home of some of his friends when an intruder broke in and began firing a pistol. Charles happened to be in the line of fire and was shot in the stomach by a bullet, often described as a "dumdum" because it exploded inside the body, causing a large amount of damage to internal organs.

Charles was hospitalized for many weeks, and he had to undergo

Beginning Again After The War

many surgical procedures to repair the damaged organs. The most serious injury was to the pancreas, an organ that produces enzymes which, if not contained, can digest other organs. He never fully recovered from the injuries, yet he was able to return to work and get married to a wonderful woman who cared for him until his premature death. He will always be remembered for his ever-present smile and the ease of making friends.

Juanita, who was called "Pru," was very possibly the most difficult of the Dixons to get close to. She was usually quiet and stayed to herself. I always felt as though she objected to me moving into her "space" in the Dixon family. She was not openly hostile but also never very warm. Unlike my ready relationships with Big Brother and Little Brother, Pru and I struggled to develop a brother-sister relationship. We always managed to be cordial, and we often visited each other throughout the years until her death.

My children, ultimately all five of them, adored their Aunt Juanita, as she would always make a big fuss over them and, of course, spoil them as aunts can do. She played a vital role in raising our children and went so far as to relocate from her home in Atlanta to Flint, Michigan, to be with us at a time we needed her help. While she and I were never really close, I am indebted to her for all she did for our family.

Pru became an excellent elementary school teacher and taught in the Flint public school system until her retirement. She married Chris Watson, one of Flint's most eligible bachelors, a very industrious and hard-working union man. Chris also contracted for outside work that kept him very busy. His death at an early age was totally unexpected, as he appeared to be in excellent health. Pru also had health problems that led to her early demise. Norma and their daughter Christel were with her to the very end.

Christel became a part of our extended family. With her husband Craig, she had a son who joined his two sons by a previous marriage, and they all became a part of the Anderson family, visiting and traveling together.

William G Anderson, DO, FACOS

Marrying Norma, moving to Atlanta, and becoming a member of the Dixon family were the smartest things I ever did in my life, even if they weren't my idea. If there was ever the necessity of proving the age-old adage of "the Lord looks after babies and fools," I am the living proof I was not a baby; I leave the conclusion to the reader.

Without Norma, it is very unlikely that I would have otherwise chosen to live in Atlanta because I was basically a small-town boy with big ambitions and no resources. Without Norma, my chances of meeting Martin Luther King Jr., her childhood neighbor, were remote, especially in that he was not yet known by more than a few outside of his immediate family. Without Norma, I would not have become a mortician and I would not have been offered a job in Montgomery, Alabama, where I met Ralph David Abernathy, and I would not have joined Dexter Avenue Baptist Church that was pastored by Rev. Vernon Johns and later Martin Luther King Jr. Little did I realize that Montgomery would become "ground zero" for the greatest Civil Rights Movement in the history of America.

Our future was beginning to be unfurled before our eyes, but we did not have the imagination, the vision, or the foresight to see what was coming. Our first child was born in Atlanta, where I first met and became friends with Martin Luther King Jr., who would later become the most significant civil rights leader of the century. Then our second child was born in Montgomery, Alabama, the last place we would have ever considered living, yet the place where we met and developed a very close friendship with Ralph David Abernathy, who would become the hand of Martin Luther King Jr. Neither of these two civil rights figures knew each other or could have anticipated that their paths would cross in future years.

I could not have planned, designed, orchestrated, or contrived such a series of events that would bring us together—Martin, Ralph, Norma, and me. This union in later years would not only be rewarding to us individually and personally but would contribute to the advancement of Black people in America and freedom-loving people the world over.

Montgomery Mortician
1947–1949

After graduation from mortuary science school, I began looking for a better job. I now had a wife, a child, and a second one on the way. My desire to get into medical school had not diminished, but the rejections had begun to pile up with little hope of acceptance. I also felt it important to stay in school if I would have any chance of ever becoming a doctor.

My job search led me to Montgomery, Alabama, where I had received an offer from J.H. Lovelace, owner of a long-established funeral home. Mr. Lovelace had inherited the business from his father, who was very successful. He had no immediate family and had never been married. He was widely known in Montgomery as the proverbial playboy, a reputation that was justly earned. He took great pride in driving his bright red Buick convertible with the top down through the Black neighborhoods. Most of what his parents had accumulated was squandered by J.H. on fast cars, prize horses, and wild parties—all of which contributed to his pleasures but ultimately to his failure to maintain and grow the funeral home business. He often spoke of his squandered life and his desire to have two sons, for he said, "If I had only one son, he will probably turn out to be no good like me, so I need two."

Despite some personal flaws, Mr. Lovelace had some good qualities, and he respected those with ambition. It was this part of his life that benefited me the most. He made me an offer that I could not turn down. I was given the opportunity to continue my college education at Alabama State College for Negroes while working as an embalmer and funeral director.

Mr. Lovelace died in his sixties of cancer of the larynx, possibly related to heavy drinking and smoking. It was my duty as the embalmer to prepare him for the funeral and burial, and I was told it was one of the best jobs of embalming that the town had ever seen.

I met some memorable people while working for Mr. Lovelace. Among them was a man called "Sonny." No one could recall how or when he got that name, nor was there much interest in discovering whether he had another name, first or last. "Sonny" was an institution at Lovelace Funeral Home, this being the only job he had had most of his life. Sonny could not read or write but took great pride in assisting with funerals. Lovelace Funeral Home also provided ambulance service. Whenever Sonny was called on to make a run, either ambulance or hearse, he would insist on the name and address being written down. This was sort of a standing joke in the funeral home because everyone knew that Sonny was illiterate. Yet the funeral home manager would always comply with Sonny's request and write down the name and address. We often wondered what Sonny did with the written note, but no one wanted to embarrass him by asking him to read it, and somehow Sonny always managed to go to the right place and bring the right body back or transport the right patient to the local hospital.

Another high point in my short life in Montgomery came when Norma and I joined Dexter Avenue Baptist Church, the church that would be later pastored by Martin Luther King Jr. But more importantly at that time, it was the church that was pastored by Vernon Johns. Reverend Johns was possibly the most brilliant, articulate, courageous, and outspoken civil rights advocate whom I have ever met. Not only was it a source of inspiration to hear Rev. Johns preach on Sunday mornings, but I had the extraordinary benefit of engaging him one-on-one in personal, private conversations in the wee hours of the morning at the funeral home.

Reverend Johns was known to be a wanderer, frequently walking the streets of Montgomery at night or early in the morning talking to anyone who would listen or who would engage him in conversation. I always looked forward to the opportunity, as my duties at the funeral home frequently required me to be there all night. When I was not busy embalming or performing other chores in the funeral home, I would be studying or eagerly awaiting the arrival of Vernon Johns. As enjoyable as those occasions were, I did not have a full appreciation of the impact they would have upon my life until years later.

Long before the Civil Rights Movement that began in 1955, Vernon Johns was openly condemning the practices of racial segregation and discrimination. He would often preach on the subject. This was a very courageous thing to do, especially in view of the fact that Dexter Avenue Baptist Church was within the shadows of the Alabama State Capitol, the cradle of the Confederacy. On one Sunday morning, Rev. Johns had posted on the marquee of the church the title of his message: "It is legal to lynch a Negro in Alabama." The town was in an uproar, both Black and White. Blacks were eager to hear the sermon, and Whites were fearful of the message and the effect it would have on the people of Montgomery. Early that Sunday morning, Vernon walked from the state capitol down Dexter Avenue to his church, where he preached to a standing-room-only audience, and without incident. He was far ahead of his time, and I have no doubt that had he been in Montgomery in 1955, or any other site where there was civil rights activity, Vernon would have been in the midst of it and assuming a leadership role.

Since I was a student at Alabama State, my wife and I first lived in government projects without the benefit of central heat, and, of course, air conditioning was unknown. It was during this time that I met a schoolmate by the name of Ralph David Abernathy, who was also an aspiring preacher. (I cannot yet explain how it was that I was constantly attracted to preachers.) Ralph became a very close friend of ours, so much so that he became the godfather to our oldest daughter, Laurita.

Our mode of transportation was a simple motor scooter that I had purchased for about $40, which was a considerable amount of money for us in the mid-1940s. Ralph enjoyed using my motor scooter and would permit me to borrow his small two-seat coupe automobile to do grocery shopping or to carry my wife and young daughter to various places.

This friendship that developed between Ralph, Norma, and me endured through college, the Civil Rights Movement, and beyond for many years, up until the time of his death.

The Return to Atlanta
1949–1952

The Lovelace Funeral Home, where I worked in Montgomery, had been the last place on the face of this earth where I had expected to find myself. But I could not turn down the opportunity of employment, taking care of my family and completing my college education. My job there survived the death of Mr. Lovelace and lasted until I graduated from Alabama State College for Negroes. However, the name "Alabama State College for Negroes" did not survive. At every opportunity, students would cover over the part of the name that identified them as Negroes. This was done over the violent objection of the president of the college, who felt it necessary to maintain that identity to preserve its funding.

As soon as I received my degree in the summer of 1949, Norma, our two children, and I moved to Atlanta to stay with Norma's mother and two brothers and sisters. I also returned to pursue a master's degree from Atlanta University while continuing my efforts to gain admission to medical school. I applied for a job in Atlanta as a teacher in the public school system. At the same time, I was offered a job at my alma mater, the Atlanta College of Mortuary Science. The choice was a no-brainer. They both paid $200 a month, but the College of Mortuary Science paid for 12 months, while the public schools only paid nine months.

Its president, B.T. Harvey, was a well-known chemistry professor at Atlanta University, and perhaps even better known as a coach, referee, and umpire for the athletic events. The dean was Samuel Pierce, a very impressive and dramatic teacher who took great pride in the mortuary science profession. In addition to teaching, he wrote extensively about the history and the art of mortuary science and was well-recognized as a very competent embalmer and restorative artist. Sam, who was quite ambitious, did not see his professional career ending as a dean of a small mortuary science college, but his ambitions were cut short as he succumbed to the ravages of a paralyzing stroke from which he never completely recovered.

The mortuary science college had a small faculty; therefore, each of us taught several courses. My first course was anatomy, but I also taught chemistry, physiology (yes, physiology for the dead) and filled in on occasion with the teaching of restorative art.

There were a number of funeral homes in the Atlanta area that were too small to hire a full-time embalmer, and therefore, they would call on the College of Mortuary Science to provide these contract services. I was frequently called to work at a number of funeral homes, and I would more often than not take the students with me to teach them the techniques of embalming.

On one occasion, I was caught up trying to hold together my teaching responsibilities, attending graduate classes at Atlanta University, and doing some embalming for independent funeral homes, and I found myself also trying to care for my two children. Laurita was quite small and enrolled in nursery school, and I had the responsibility of taking her from home to school. On one of my busiest days, I stopped by my office with Laurita in the mortuary science building. Rita was with me in my office when I was summoned to the front office for a call to go to Marietta, a suburb of Atlanta, to embalm a body. I neglected to return to my office but

The Return to Atlanta

hastened to my automobile and to Marietta to the embalming. Some hours later, I received a call from one of my friends on the faculty, who advised me that my daughter was in my office sitting very quietly in a soft chair where I had left her several hours earlier. I panicked, for in my haste, I left her in my office. She proved to be much more sensible and courageous than her father in that, without a complaint or a whimper, she sat quietly and obediently where I had left her until a friend whom she recognized picked her up for me.

At night, I taught at a public high school, Booker T. Washington High, a job I got through a fraternity connection. A frat brother was the principal. I taught English—yes, I said English—and that, too, was a joke because I knew little about sentence structure and even less about syntax. My lack of knowledge did not stop me from teaching. It was just a matter of staying one chapter ahead of my students.

My weekends were somewhat free, so I joined the young adult choir of Wheat Street Baptist Church, one of the leading churches of Atlanta. You might have guessed: I could not sing. My lack of ability never seemed to interfere with my trying anything and everything. Under the direction of L.C. Mann, a musician, music teacher, and choir director, the choir was exceptionally good. Our reputation spread to the radio community, resulting in an invitation to sing in a regularly scheduled Sunday morning religious broadcast service. This was the beginning of my career in radio.

The Wheat Street Choir and its announcer, Ray McIver, a high school English teacher with a golden voice, attained celebrity status after a few appearances. One Sunday morning, as we were preparing for our broadcast, our announcer failed to show up. Our director asked if any member of the choir could read. You may think that's an odd question, but please understand that reading was not essential to singing. I volunteered to fill in for the missing announcer.

Somewhat to my surprise, there were people in the radio audience who listened to our choir singing and on this particular occasion, heard me as the announcer. One such person in the audience was Ken Knight, a program director for the only Black-owned and operated radio station in the nation at that time. At the end of the broadcast, he called the station, requested to speak to me, and asked if I was interested in being a radio announcer. I told him that I had no such intentions, had never even given it any thought, and that I was merely filling in for the regular announcer who was unable to make the scheduled broadcast for that Sunday morning. He thanked me for taking the time to speak to him and indicated that if I changed my mind and decided to try out radio, to please contact him. He gave me his name, phone number, and address.

Again, not having my weekends filled, I eventually decided to give Knight a call and to visit him at the "Good WERD" station. Ken invited me to read a few lines on the air to test my voice. He liked what he heard and offered me a job on air, working on weekends, at a time I could set myself. I accepted the offer to become the announcer on a variety show, which aired on Saturday and Sunday afternoons. Much to my surprise I was paired with James Patrick, better known as "Alley Pat." Alley Pat had a well-known variety show that he always promoted as coming from "the hole." He and I made quite a team, with me often being his straight man. I progressed to having a show on Sunday morning independent of Alley Pat, where I played classical and mood music and read poetry, of all things. Imagine me, reading poetry. This experience in radio proved to be quite beneficial to me in that it offered opportunities for employment that later would help to keep me in medical school.

By the way, Knight had the distinction of being the only program director who could not read a single commercial without making a mistake. This was a standing joke around the radio station that often led to friendly wagers around the station.

Life in Atlanta was unlike anything I had experienced. To see Blacks in business and politics was a new experience for me. Atlanta had often been referred to as the "New York of the South," for Negroes had privileges as well as businesses not to be found in any other city south of the Mason-Dixon Line. "Sweet Auburn Avenue," eloquently described by John Wesley Dobbs, the unofficial mayor of

The Return to Atlanta

Atlanta and the Grand Warden of the Prince Hall Masons, was one of the two main streets that were lined with Black-owned businesses; the other was West Hunter Street. These famous streets boasted Black insurance companies, banks, hotels, office buildings, theaters, pool halls, beauty parlors, and barbershops. In addition, there were affluent suburbs that extended from West Hunter across East Lake to Center Road. Walter H. "Chief" Aiken had built the Waluhaje Apartment Complex, the first high-rise luxury apartment building for Negroes in the city.

Simpson Road, one of the main roads through the Black neighborhood, was the gateway to multiple housing subdivisions where you would find the homes of many of the more affluent Blacks. There were also nightclubs and the Lincoln Country Club. The American Legion night club was very popular, and as a veteran I became a member and frequent visitor. In addition to entertainment that included the likes of Gladys Knight and the Pips before her celebrity status, there were also games of chance. The American Legion, not unlike other clubs in the area, had gaming in the form of slot machines, although it was not legal. The American Legion, as other clubs, would be periodically raided by police. However, we always seemed to know when the raid would take place and had ample time to move the slot machines from the public area into private rooms that were remarkably never entered during the raids.

The Lincoln County Club had a nine-hole golf course that wound its way around a cemetery. While I did not yet play golf, I did have the opportunity of visiting the club on an occasion when world-class boxer Joe Louis was in town. Louis was an avid golfer, even though he rarely won anything on the course. To maintain his financial viability, he needed to continue to box and not to rely on golf.

In the few years that we lived in Atlanta, we came to appreciate the fact that Blacks there had a unique opportunity to be exposed to the best in education and culture, as both could be found in abundance within the Atlanta University system. It was not an exaggeration to say that Atlanta University was the seat of superior Black intellect in the world. The university system with its colleges—Morehouse, Spelman, Clark, and Morris Brown—produced more Black educators, industrialists, business and professional people than any comparable educational system in the world. There was also Gammon Theological Seminary, Atlanta School of Social Work, the Atlanta College of Mortuary Science—all of these contributed to Atlanta being a major academic center.

To live in Atlanta in the middle of the 20th century was an amazing revelation of what a Black person could become. There was an abundance of professionals including lawyers, doctors, builders, engineers, financiers, bankers, economists and aspiring politicians. Atlanta was also the home of the Atlanta Life Insurance Company, one of the major Black-owned insurance companies in America. There were also offices for North Carolina Mutual Life Insurance Company, Pilgrim, Afro-American, and other smaller insurance companies. There were Black businessmen the likes of which could not be found anywhere else in the country. Names such as Yates, Milton, Blayton, Calhoun, Paschal, Herndon, McClendon, Hackney, Dobbs, Walden, Aikens, Borders, King and Anderson were household names that spelled successful Blacks.

C.R. Yates and L.D. Milton were well known as entrepreneurs, businessmen and bankers. Milton was president of one of the few Black-owned banks in the United States. Together they also owned drugstores.

J.B. Blayton, who owned the radio station (WERD) where I worked, was an enterprising businessman, the first and one of the few Black certified public accountants in the entire South. Among other businesses, Blayton owned an accounting company, business and electronics schools, and was a major stockholder in Citizens Trust Bank. He was highly regarded among the business and professional people in Georgia.

Then there was John Calhoun, one of the few Black political leaders in Atlanta who was registered as a Republican. This was out of the ordinary because in the state of Georgia, the Republican Party

The Return to Atlanta

was almost nonexistent. The political primaries were all White and Democrat. When Blacks first gained the right to vote in isolated areas in Georgia, their only choice was to vote Democratic. Our choices would often be only between two racists, and we would choose the lesser of two evils.

Paschal Brothers Restaurant on West Hunter was a place where, into the early 1950s, one could get a fried chicken sandwich that constituted a meal. The 50-cent sandwich consisted of one quarter of chicken with lettuce and tomato that was more than enough for one person. The brothers later operated a hotel with a restaurant and nightclub that became very successful.

My favorite vision of what a Black man could be, was H.H. Anderson. Dr. Anderson was known as the "midnight doctor," in that it was not unusual for him to spend the entire night in his office on Sweet Auburn Street. His office was in one of two Black-owned office buildings, adjacent to a Black-owned hotel, The Royal, and only a short distance away from a Black nightclub, The Royal Peacock.

Dr. Anderson was one of the most brilliant doctors in Atlanta. He never was known to be in a hurry. He had gained a reputation of never going home, taking off his clothes, or going to bed. He had the apparent capacity of going for weeks on end rejuvenated and refreshed only by brief naps. It was thought that he could take a nap while a thermometer was in a patient's mouth getting warm or while a traffic light changed from red to green. On at least one occasion, he was arrested because there was a suspicion of him being drunk and falling asleep at the wheel. When it was discovered that this was his style of living, he was promptly released.

Dr. Anderson was not only our personal physician but was also a friend. He cared for Norma during one of her pregnancies and we would often stop by to visit if we saw his light on after going to a movie. One could expect to spend several hours in his office before being seen, even though you might arrive as late as 11 p.m.

Williams Holmes Borders, M.L. "Daddy" King, B.J. Johnson, and Roland Smith were well-known preachers in the Atlanta area. They were the best of friends and found great joy in personal confrontation. They would often engage each other in moving debates that bordered on arguments. Only a group of preachers who deeply loved each other could have possibly survived such encounters.

Reverend Borders was known as the radio preacher and had written and published two widely read books entitled *Seven Minutes at the Mike* and *I Am Somebody*. He was pastor of the Wheat Street Baptist Church, which served as a venue for Black civil rights advocates long before the Montgomery bus boycott of 1955. It was at Wheat Street where I had the opportunity of hearing Ralph Bunch and others who were in the forefront of the advancement of Blacks in America. Reverend Borders, more than any other orator, quite possibly had the greatest influence on the development of my comfort in speaking before large groups. In addition to having an imposing feature, he had a commanding voice and a captivating persona. He was most impressive and would speak to a church filled to capacity every Sunday. He was also in demand as a teacher. For many years he was on the faculty of Morehouse College.

"Daddy" King, the father of Martin Luther King Jr., was the pastor of Ebenezer Baptist Church, a church that had been founded by his father-in-law. Daddy King was a highly regarded pastor and community leader long before the civil rights era of the 1950s.

B.J. Johnson was a fiery and colorful preacher who had the ability to stir the emotions of his congregation into an absolute frenzy. His preaching was often enhanced by the music of his very talented wife, who played the piano and directed the choir. This musical talent was handed down to succeeding generations of Johnsons.

Roland Smith was the pastor of a church in Little Rock, Arkansas. That appeared out of the ordinary for one who lived in Atlanta, but he was able to make the trip as often as necessary. He also was editor of the *Georgia Baptist* newspaper. While he carried the title, it was my mother-in-law, Mary Dixon, who in fact functioned as the editor. I was frequently the editorial writer. This was my first experience in writing for a publication but served me quite well in later years.

The Return to Atlanta

Roland Smith later married Mary Dixon and he became my step-father-in-law.

During my stay in Atlanta, Martin Luther King Jr. and I became friends and were involved in some of the activities in and around Morehouse College where he was attending. Together we assisted in the establishment of a youth chapter of the NAACP (National Association for the Advancement of Colored People) on the Morehouse campus. It was during this time I began to sense the qualities that Martin had that would eventually enable him to become an outstanding preacher and leader. At no time did I anticipate how far he would go as a leader and certainly did not anticipate that one day he would challenge the conscience of this nation and the world and become the recipient of a Nobel Peace Prize. Martin graduated from Morehouse College and went on to study at the Crozer Theological Seminary in Chester, Pennsylvania. Our paths would not cross again until several years later with the advent of the Montgomery bus boycott.

I never gave up on my quest to become a physician and continued to apply regularly. Then a chance meeting of Willie Joe Reese, D.O. (Doctor of Osteopathy) changed my life forever and started me on the path to become an osteopathic physician. There are only two physicians recognized in America, allopath (MD) and osteopath (DO). The former came to America from Europe and was more commonplace at the time. Osteopathic medicine was actually developed in America, with education and training focused on holistic, or whole-person care. I wasn't sure it would happen in my lifetime, but it is now one of the fastest-growing segments of healthcare in America, with 1 out of every 3 physicians now graduating from an osteopathic medical school.

I shall be eternally grateful to my father, without whom I would never have met Dr. Reese nor heard of the osteopathic profession. My father was a close friend and fraternity brother of Dr. Reese. When Dr. Reese learned of my interest in medicine and the difficulty that I had gaining admission to a medical school, he offered his assistance.

William G Anderson, DO, FACOS

At first, when my father told me of his offer, I turned it down. I told him I wanted to be a "real doctor." Osteopathic medicine was unknown to me at the time, and to everyone I knew. Then I decided to find out for myself.

A visit to Dr. Reese's office immediately changed my mind and my way of thinking about osteopathic medicine. Dr. Reese had the biggest, most successful family practice in Albany, Georgia. He was doing everything the other Black doctors—the MDs—in the South were doing, but on a larger scale. I said to my father, "That's just what I want to do."

In as kind and gentle a manner as he could muster, my father said, "l tried to tell you that, hard head" (or words to that effect). I got the message and charted a new course.

Transforming into an Osteopathic Physician
1952–1956

My application to the Des Moines Still College of Osteopathy was accepted, and I was invited for an interview. My father's friend, Dr. Willie Joe Reese, had fulfilled his promise to contact Dean John B. Shumaker, Ph.D., and ask that consideration be given to me for admission. I was met by the dean and immediately subjected to the required examinations to determine my eligibility. I was given the Ohio Reading Comprehension Examination (ORCE) and the Minnesota Multiphasic Personality Inventory (MMPI). Both of these I passed satisfactorily and was granted admission to the college. I was ecstatic. Finally, I had the opportunity to become a physician. I had no idea how I could afford the tuition and support a family, but I returned to Atlanta with the good news that I had been accepted and would be starting school in the fall.

Because of our limited resources Norma, expecting our third child, stayed in Atlanta with our two older children, Rita and Gil. My plan was to return to Atlanta at every opportunity— Thanksgiving, Christmas, winter break and summer for visits. Mother Mary was there to help and willing to do what she could, and of course, my mother was there saying, "Just go on, William. We will figure out a way."

When I left Atlanta, I had a total of $600. This constituted all my earthly possessions, as we had sold my automobile and whatever furnishings we had accumulated to raise enough money to start me in school. Fortunately, I was entitled to benefits under the G.I. Bill—tuition and a small monthly subsistence that would last for one semester. Beyond that point I had no idea how we would possibly survive.

When I arrived in Des Moines as a freshman student at the Des Moines Still College of Osteopathy, I was filled with great anxiety and enthusiasm, for I felt as though finally my dreams and ambitions of being a doctor would be fulfilled. I was greeted very warmly as I entered the lobby of the college by a resident in internal medicine, Murray Goldstein. Murray introduced himself and escorted me around the college, showing me all the various classrooms and introducing me to as many of the faculty and administration as were in the building. That kind gesture endeared me to Murray for life. This act of kindness would come to typify Murray, who later became the first osteopathic physician to receive a permanent appointment at the National Institutes of Health, where he headed the section on neurological diseases. Murray was highly regarded and highly respected as a brilliant physician.

I found a very kind landlady, Lena Reeves, who had for many years given assistance to college students attending universities in the area. She took me in and provided me with a room and one meal a day. I shared a bathroom with other students in the house.

It was this same Mrs. Reeves who, with her keen power of observation, recognized that I was absolutely miserable and incapable of concentrating and studying without my wife and children. She found a way to move me into a larger room that would accommodate my whole family. She arranged the furniture in such a manner that we could laughingly refer to it as a bedroom, sitting room, dining room, kitchen, and nursery—all in the confines of one room. I did not

Transforming into an Osteopathic Physician

complain, nor did Norma when she saw these makeshift arrangements, for together, we had a vision, and we knew that this was the only means to reach our goal. In February 1953, a third child, Vale Jeanita, was born, and then we were five.

To support my family, I sought employment. I secured the job of embalmer for the school when it became known that I was licensed. What I had learned at the Atlanta College of Mortuary Science I applied to preparing cadavers for dissection in the anatomy laboratory. I was somewhat innovative when I discovered the formaldehyde was very offensive and pungent and caused many students to have difficulties being in the laboratory. The anatomy professor asked if I could prepare suitable embalming chemicals that would not yield such an offensive odor. I set out to develop such a formula, using as a base primarily ethyl alcohol rather than formaldehyde for the preservation. That formula was used many years thereafter. It's one that I never patented, but it was generally known that it was mine, notwithstanding the fact that it was later claimed by others. In addition, a new anatomy professor, a retired Army colonel, discovered that I previously taught anatomy and promoted me to become a prosector, one who teaches anatomy by demonstration for the medical students. I was almost able to make ends meet with my two jobs at the college.

My experience as a radio announcer opened a door of opportunity at KWDM, a small, family-owned radio station struggling for survival. George Webber was the owner and manager. He was a man of limited resources that he used extremely well to hold the station together. Mr. Webber had the unusual ability to get people to work very hard, for long hours and for little pay. It was only by his strong will and determination that KWDM stayed on the air, and there were intervals when it was not broadcasting because bills had not been paid.

As employees we would on occasion be called on to contribute our salaries to pay the light bill or the rent. On one occasion, I presented my check to the bank to be cashed, only to discover that

Mr. Webber did not have sufficient funds to cover the check. I asked my boss to make the check good only to leave lending him money to pay more of the station's bills. He had a persuasive manner that made it difficult to say "no."

My employment at KWDM came about as a result of some unconventional negotiations. To better understand these negotiations, we need to review the conditions that existed in Des Moines in 1952. Des Moines was geographically far removed from rural Georgia, but racially very close with almost as much segregation and discrimination in one as there was in the other. The only difference was the absence of "Colored" and "White" signs. There were no legal barriers to voting, but few Blacks participated in the process. Many restaurants and bars were off-limits to Blacks. Schools, churches, recreational centers and housing were as segregated as anywhere else in the country.

Des Moines also had its "Harlem." It was called Center Street and was where most of the Blacks congregated for social life and business. There I found a Black-owned drugstore, cafeteria, barbershop and the ever-present pool hall. The drugstore was owned and operated by a preacher who was a social activist. He was always a willing participant in demonstrations against the racist actions of some Whites in Des Moines. He was the leader in the protest against Babe's Pizza Parlor, which refused Blacks service. He was also an outspoken opponent of other institutions that practiced racial discrimination. There were a few Black professionals, educators, physicians, dentists, and lawyers, most of whom were respected in their professional activities, but yet were subjected to the same practices of racial segregation.

There had never been a Black radio announcer there, and of course, with television being in its infancy, there was never a thought of a Black being on TV. There were a few Blacks in entertainment, and they could only make guest appearances on radio and television.

KWDM had a single radio program that played ethnic music, in 15-minute segments for one hour one day a week. The program was

Transforming into an Osteopathic Physician

losing money and about to be taken off the air. I heard of this plan and decided to try to use my radio experience in Atlanta to land a job in radio in Des Moines. "Unheard of ... never will happen ... there is no place for Blacks in radio in Des Moines ... never will be an audience ... not enough Blacks in Des Moines to support a Black radio announcer"—these were but a few of the negative words that I heard. I am certain that there were many more and some not so charitable.

I went to meet Mr. Webber and made him an offer that was hard for him to refuse. I said to him, "I understand that you are taking the Ethnic Music Hour off because it is not making any money."

He confirmed my statement and reinforced it with "It has not and will not ever make any money."

I said, "I will do the program for nothing. I will go out and sell advertisements, write the scripts, select the music, operate the controls, and be my own engineer. If the program doesn't make any money, don't pay me."

He reacted in shock. He said, "Are you crazy?"

I said, "I would like to give it a try as I have experience in radio." He then said, "If you are crazy enough to do that, I am crazy enough to give you a chance."

He gave me one hour, one day a week from 6 p.m. to 7 p.m. The program grew practically overnight, as Des Moines was hungry for a music variety show with some color (no pun intended). The program expanded in a few weeks to four hours every night, 8 p.m. to midnight. I also worked as much as I could on Saturdays and some Sunday mornings.

I made money for Mr. Webber and the meager wage that he paid me helped me to stay in school and support my family. Ultimately, my radio show was a variety show, but I also did sports and news and, as was customary in those days in small radio stations, I was also the engineer. I selected the records, I played the records, and I operated the radio console, selected and edited the news, and on occasion would go out on site for play-by-play broadcasts of basketball games.

I did this while attending class daily from 8 a.m. to 6 p.m. and studying from about 1 a.m. until class the following morning. This left little time for sleep, a luxury that I could only indulge occasionally on weekends. There were many weekdays when I failed to take off my clothes to go to bed. I was fortunate in that several of my classmates were similarly situated in that they needed to work while going to school and would wait until I got off work to study together. Together we were able to survive.

It was the spring of 1953. I was now well established as an advanced freshman student. My third child had been born and my family was more comfortably situated in an apartment house. This was a significant move in that now we had two large rooms, a living-dining area with a kitchen nook and a bedroom. And we had the good fortune of sharing a floor in this apartment building with very friendly neighbors.

I successfully completed the first year and found myself to be in the top 10 percent of my classmates. Now my task was how to earn enough money during the summer to return to classes in the fall.

With the aid of Dean Shumaker, I was able to find employment at a manufacturing company that was owned by one of his friends. I was initially assigned a workstation on a metal press, where my job was to stamp out metal parts. This was very monotonous, so I began to explore opportunities to relieve boredom in this job by adding some excitement and innovation. This took the form of accelerating the press process and increasing production. This was to the dismay of the union workers, and I was promptly warned by the union steward to cease and desist from increasing production as it would impact on the union's negotiation with management. I thus reverted back to the boredom of a press operator.

The owner of the manufacturing company learned of my ambition, removed me from the press, and assigned me duties on the warehouse dock where I mixed and filled orders for chemicals. Suddenly, with practically no training, I became a chemical engineer. The title was somewhat of an exaggeration, because I merely had to mix what I was instructed and needed to have no knowledge about

Transforming into an Osteopathic Physician

the chemicals I was mixing, or what the end product would be. If this experience of working in a factory taught me anything, it was that this was not what I wanted to do with the rest of my life, reinforcing my intention to become a physician.

Charles A. Murphy and David L. McSwain had applied to Des Moines Still College of Osteopathy, and were interviewed and accepted. They were referred to me for help in getting relocated. It was customary that a new Black student would be directed to another Black student to help with finding a place to stay and to teach them the unofficial rules, especially as related to matters of race. By the time Chuck and Dave arrived, racial barriers had not been knocked down, so it was important for them to know where and how far to go without running into a racial brick wall. After the first six months at Still College, and in the city of Des Moines, I knew my place as a Black man from the Deep South. I had tested and found many places where we were not welcomed.

Immediately I knew that Dave, Chuck, and I had much in common, starting with the fact that none of us had any money nor did we have any idea how we would possibly survive four years of medical school. But we soon learned that we were all determined and would find a way if given the opportunity.

I invited them to my apartment and mentioned I was in the process of arranging to rent a small house on the east side of Des Moines. They were most eager to live with us, especially since they had sampled Norma's cooking.

They initiated discussion around the cost of room and board. My response was, "We are all in this together, trying to survive. Let's place all of the bills in one pot, and whoever has the money to pay for it, will pay."

I did not know how to charge someone with no money, and it was kind of comforting to know that at least two of my schoolmates had as little, if not less, than me. The arrangement worked; we shared all the expenses, including the cost of an automobile. I found a 12-year-old two-door Dodge with the grill smashed in and the body had been repainted flat black. The car had two positive features: it ran well enough to provide transportation for the three of us and it had an electric block heater that assured its starting in the severe cold that was typical in Des Moines. The automobile served its purpose well. We were able to get to and from school, to and from work, and occasionally Dave and Chuck would use the car to go out on dates. Granted, you could not get in and out of the same door, but this was only a minor inconvenience.

Later we had the good fortune of meeting the Lewis family, who epitomized "salt of the earth." There was Dorothy and Woodrow, who had three children, Charles, Dave, and Debbie. The Lewises were also members of Corinthian Baptist Church. We had never met anyone outside of the immediate family who was more loving, kind, understanding, and willing to help us get through school. The Lewises' shared everything: their home, their food, their friendship and their love. That friendship has endured for more than 50 years.

We soon learned that they had a house close to the college, and the rent was low enough that the three of us could pool our resources to pay it. It was a stretch to call it a two-bedroom house; it was really a one-bedroom with an attic that we turned into a second bedroom. But who could complain? We were all struggling to survive medical school.

Norma and I had the lower floor with a bedroom, living room, dining area and a kitchen. Laurita and Gil slept in double deck bunk beds in the living room, and Jeannie, our baby, slept in a crib near Norma and me. We ate together when we could, and it never seemed to be very crowded except at bathroom time. Seven people sharing one small bathroom occasionally posed a problem. But none of us could afford to complain, so we didn't.

Norma cooked for everyone and became the mother of us all. Without her loving, tender, compassionate care, none of us would have survived. She went so far as to cook the favorite meals of Chuck and Dave, making them feel even more at home. Chuck's favorite was homemade cake that he would hungrily devour with a glass of milk

Transforming into an Osteopathic Physician

before dinner. You could not find a pepper sauce too hot for Dave. He tried them all, but he would never admit that it was too spicy—notwithstanding the profuse perspiration that we noticed as he was eating it, nor did he report the outcome on the next day.

We were a family, first out of necessity, but then it grew into a welcomed privilege. We shared everything: food, clothes, cars, books and what little money we had. It was not at all unusual for Chuck or Dave to diaper the baby or rock the young ones to sleep or get up during the night to meet their needs.

As Dave and Chuck approached their third and fourth years of medical school, their interest turned to marriage. After marriage, each one moved out, leaving the two-bedroom house. We occasionally had other renters to share the expenses, but never again any like Chuck and Dave, who were more like brothers to Norma and me and uncles to our children. That friendship never ended.

Into my third year of osteopathic medical school, I found it a decided advantage to develop friendships with some of my classmates, especially those who shared my concerns of survival—that is, survival in the classroom and survival at home with a wife and children. John Gier, Buddy Beville, Joe Schmidt, Mike Warhola and Joe Battersby were among those whom I found to be compatible with my necessary patterns of study. Because my job in radio lasted until midnight, it was necessary to find study partners who could start about 1 a.m. and be prepared to study as long as necessary to keep up. We would go for weeks without getting a full night's sleep except on the weekend.

Studying with John Gier proved to be most helpful in that he had befriended a lady who worked at the major department store in town. She had as much interest in John surviving the medical school career as any of us. We all believed that her interest and ambitions extended beyond John getting a D.O. degree. Martha always made certain we had plenty of hot coffee, snacks, cookies, candy and nuts, she watched to make sure we did not take too many breaks. She was quick to say, "Back to the books!"

I found the most lasting study partner to be Buddy Beville, who had been a pharmacist before enrolling in osteopathic medical school. He was able to find employment as a pharmaceutical representative in Des Moines. His after-school duties required him to call on practicing physicians. This he would do soon after class until about 11 p.m. and after he made out his reports, he'd be ready to start studying by midnight. Our schedules for study aligned extremely well.

Joe Battersby worked in a chemical factory between attending class and studying. It was evident to all in the classroom that Joe worked in chemicals, because they would cling to his clothes and sometimes would bring tears to your eyes with their pungent, penetrating odors. We all tolerated the atmosphere around Joe, for we had much in common in trying to balance medical school and earning a living.

Des Moines Still College had no shortage of memorable teachers. Carrie Gillespie was professor of gross anatomy. Anatomy traditionally had been scheduled as the first class, the first hour the first day of medical school. It was usual in most medical schools that there was an attrition rate that varied anywhere from 10 to 25 percent. Still College was no different except that the highest attrition occurred the first class of the first day, which was taught, coincidentally, by Professor Gillespie. Her greeting to the incoming freshman class was "You are six weeks behind already." Needless to say, that got our attention. She went on to write on the blackboard in bold letters "WORK: That is the yeast that raises the dough." Carrie's greeting was less of a warm friendly welcome than a frightening snarl. If her intention was to threaten and intimidate the freshmen, she readily succeeded. She had a reputation for carrying the highest academic mortality rate of

Transforming into an Osteopathic Physician

any of the professors. Despite her demeanor and never-ceasing pressure, Carrie was one of the finest anatomists that I have ever known. She knew anatomy not only from the textbooks but could dissect in great detail every body part, including every nerve and blood vessel. She was an extraordinary anatomist.

We learned how to interpret, if not speak, Chinese in our class in bacteriology and parasitology. It was taught by a Chinese professor who was brilliant but had difficulty with the English language, or more precisely, we had difficulty interpreting his version of the English language. We soon learned that "frees," "musketoes," and "budds" were respectively, "fleas," "mosquitoes," and "bugs." Once we became accustomed to the way he spoke we came to the realization that he was an excellent teacher. Dr. Hsie later enrolled in the college and studied to become an osteopathic physician. As fate would have it, I was teaching anatomy and in a reversal of role, the student became the teacher. I learned two things in this role reversal: first, a teacher can be intimidated by a former student, and second, reformed teachers do not take kindly to failure, especially when they're on the receiving end. Following an anatomy exam, I told Dr. Hsie in jest, that he had failed my quiz, which promptly ended our longstanding friendly relationship. I came to realize that Dr. Hsie did not have an appreciation for my style of humor. In fact, he was a very good student and satisfactorily passed my anatomy class.

I did not escape the embarrassment and humiliation of segregation and discrimination by going to Des Moines. These were very much alive there in the early fifties, as many places of business would not serve people of color. To my amazement, even in the academic and administration building of the Still College of Osteopathy, I was confronted with these specters.

First, I was denied admission to the Square and Compass Club, a club of the Masons. I became a Mason while a student at Alabama

State College. However, I was told by members of the Square and Compass Club that since I belonged to a Clandestine Order of the Masons, I was therefore ineligible for membership in their group. I also learned that there were several Greek fraternities at the college that had never accepted a Black member.

To reinforce the segregationist climate at the college, Dean Shumaker advised me not to socialize with any of the White females at the school or in the city of Des Moines. This, he told me, was a friendly gesture to avoid any future problems. This admonishment would later become a major crisis for me. It was at one of the college's official social functions, a dance, where I was confronted with a serious dilemma that forced me to make a crisis decision. At this function I was called on to dance with Ms. Sandine, who was an instructor in biochemistry. Ms. Sandine, who was White, for some reason after having a couple of cocktails, elected to send a message to me by one of my classmates that she wanted to dance with me. Remembering what the dean had told me about socializing with White women and yet recognizing that Ms. Sandine held my fate in her hands as to whether or not I would satisfactorily pass the course in biochemistry, I had to make a quick decision. I braced myself and elected to run the risk of ignoring Dean Shumaker's advice. I danced with Ms. Sandine to the amazement and astonishment of a number of my classmates and others of the college family who were present at this official social function. To my surprise and I'm certain to many others, there were never any repercussions, and it was the beginning of the end of official segregation at social functions at Des Moines Still College of Osteopathy.

I had accepted these segregationist conditions, as my primary motivation was to get an education and to get a degree so I could practice medicine. I did not go to Des Moines to initiate my own private civil rights movement. Notwithstanding the racist climate, there were classmates who readily accepted me for who I was and agreed that we would study together and support each other through these four years of medical school. Student Doctors Gier, Battersby,

Transforming into an Osteopathic Physician

Beville, Goldberg and others befriended me, and we created a pact that said we would go nowhere in Des Moines where we all could not go together. We studied together, we ate together, and we often slept at each other's homes; we were a family.

I successfully completed the first two years of osteopathic medicine yet to be confronted with segregation and discrimination in the clinics. The clinic staff only assigned Black patients to me until I complained, whereupon they very reluctantly changed the policy, and I began to get a few White patients.

An Osteopathic Intern in Michigan
1956–1957

Flint Osteopathic Hospital (FOH) in Michigan had the reputation of being one of the best training hospitals for osteopathic medical students in the country. It was second only to the "Mecca," Detroit Osteopathic, and perhaps on par with Doctor's Hospital in Columbus, Ohio.

FOH had never had a Black physician on staff or in training. The unwritten and unspoken policy of racism was evident. By the end of my second year as a medical student, Dean Shumaker was well aware of my medical knowledge and also my ability to adapt and get along with people who had little experience interacting with Blacks at a professional level. After hearing of my request to go to FOH for my training, the dean immediately knew that I would be rejected as soon as they discovered my racial identity. So, he took the unusual step of first placing a call to the administrator of FOH, advising him of my request and alerting him to the fact that I was Black. The administrator was somewhat liberal and was convinced by Dean Shumaker that allowing me to study there was the right thing to do. He reluctantly agreed to accept me as an extern (clinical clerk). He figured that not much damage could be done with me as a medical student, acting primarily as an observer and not actually doing patient care.

But my ambition exceeded the externship, and I soon applied for the internship. That application opened up another can of worms: To do the internship, I would have to be involved in patient care. This was not something that the administration could decide. It was necessary that I be approved by the House Staff Training Committee, which selected all interns and residents. Under ordinary circumstances, the action of the House Staff Training Committee was perfunctory. My case was different, to say the least. I was required to make a personal appearance before the entire committee in a special session at the Durant Hotel in Flint to convince them that I deserved to be an intern at FOH. The issues of concern did not relate to my scholastic ability, for I was consistently in the top 10 percent of my class, and all of my evaluations on clinical rotations were well above average. The concern was my color. Finding no legitimate reason to deny my application, one very outspoken committee member, Dr. Allen Silverstone, made a motion that I be accepted on the spot. If there were any that might have objected, it would have been most difficult to find a justification for my rejection, especially with me sitting there. I was accepted and soon thereafter was an intern at my chosen hospital, FOH.

Early in my internship, racism reared its ugly head. Patients were usually assigned on a rotating basis to all of the externs and interns. I noticed that my classmates were getting assigned patients, and I was not, so I inquired about the reason at the admissions office. I was told that the administrator had advised them to tell patients as they were being admitted, "We have a colored intern, but you do not have to see him." Upon hearing this, I immediately went to the office administrator, Keith Bowker, and told him how much I appreciated the fact that he accepted me as an intern, but that I very much resented the fact that he was apologizing for having accepted me by giving patients the option to reject me because of my race. I made a pact with Mr. Bowker. If any patient ever objected to my care I would withdraw, and he would not even have to ask that I not take care of the patient. I would do it voluntarily.

I was at Flint Osteopathic Hospital for a year and three months. During that time, only one White patient objected, and he got the very best care of any patient that had ever been in that hospital. I was determined that I would win this patient over. Every time he would cough, sneeze or grunt, I would be at his bedside. But when I would attempt to administer to him, he would literally break out in a rash. His prejudice was deeply rooted.

After a few days he was discharged to go home. By this time, everyone in the hospital knew of my determination to win him over, and many were eager to hear about my failure to do so. He summoned me to his bedside; there was something that he wanted to tell me. What he said to me was very shocking yet understandable. He said that when he was a baby a big Black woman swooped him up out of his stroller and embraced him vigorously over his objection and frightened him terribly. He said that he was emotionally scarred from that point on and every time that he was in the presence of a Black person, he would react as though he was being literally crushed. I understood his psychological trauma and I appreciated the fact that he shared it with me as it indicated that it had nothing to do with me personally, or me as a member of the Black race, or the care that I was giving, but he had an emotional trauma that he was incapable of overcoming.

On another occasion, I was assigned to the OB service that was very busy in delivering babies, predominantly of White patients. It was late at night, and I was the only intern on duty. A man brought his wife in while she was in active labor, and of course I had the responsibility of examining her and caring for her during her labor until the time of delivery. The husband protested loudly, "I do not want any nigger taking care of my wife!"

The nursing supervisor immediately called Dr. Allen Corbet, chief of obstetrical services. Dr. Corbet, a highly respected obstetrician and chairman of the department, met with the irate husband

and advised him that not only was I the best qualified intern in the hospital to take care of his wife, but that I was also the only intern on obstetrical services. Either I could take care of his wife in labor or he could take his wife out of the hospital. I shall be eternally grateful to Allen Corbet for taking such a strong stand. Needless to say, this obstetrical patient got the very best OB care that she could have received, and we heard no more about the complaints of the husband.

I successfully completed the internship at Flint Osteopathic Hospital and applied for residency in surgery at the same institution. I was summarily denied. A close friend and staff physician of FOH later told me that I had been blackballed by a member of the surgery staff because of my race.

However, I was offered the opportunity to stay in practice in Flint. I was to be supported by a group of surgeons who indicated that I should not bury myself in the Black neighborhood but establish a practice on a border street where I would be able to receive both Black and White patients. The offer was very tempting, so much so that I was about to accept, until my wife, Norma, who has a phenomenal memory for things that she wants to remember, reminded me of a pledge that I had made years earlier. My pledge was that if I should ever become a doctor, I would return to Georgia to practice where I was needed. This decision, urged on me by Norma, turned out to be one of the best that I have ever made in my entire life, second only to another decision that she also urged me to make, and that was to marry her.

Had that decision not been made, we would not have become a part of history as leaders in the most important Civil Rights Movement in America in the 20th century. There would not have been the demonstrations, the marches, the mass meetings and the experience of voluntarily going to jail for what we considered a just cause. Martin Luther King Jr. and Ralph David Abernathy would not have become such an intimate part of our lives. Our lives would not have embraced Wyatt Walker, Andrew Young, Bernice Johnson Reagon,

An Osteopathic Intern in Michigan

Jackie Robinson or many thousands of others that joined us in the Albany Movement. That decision continues to have a lasting effect on our lives and what we have become. To be an active participant in such a significant historical event is something that one can only dream of. It happened because of the decision that we made (more accurately, Norma) in Flint, Michigan.

A Physician in Albany
1957–1963

Now with a degree in osteopathic medicine, a completed internship, and a license, it was time to start looking for a place to practice.

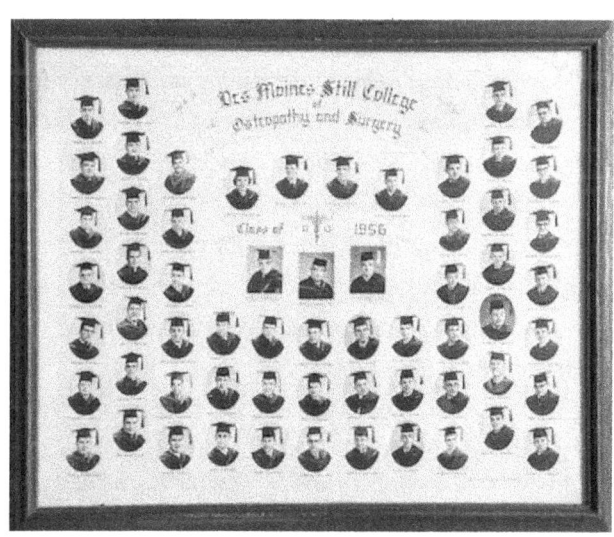

William G Anderson, DO, FACOS

Norma and I with our four children temporarily moved in with my parents and sister, Dorothy, in Americus. This arrangement was to be for only a short period of time because I was eager to start in practice, pay off some debt and start out my new life as a practicing physician. I did not want to rush the search for what I considered to be the ideal spot, for I felt it was time to settle down, plant some roots, and become a part of a community. Norma and I had been married for 11 years and had lived in seven places. It was time to get a home and some permanence.

My mother of necessity was patient with me in making this decision, but her patience grew thin when I made the mistake of telling her that while I was procrastinating, I was losing $100 a day in potential income. She was absolutely astounded. She, who had taught school for many years at $40 a month, had never known anyone in her entire life that had made as much as $100 a day. She urged me to get set up in practice as soon as possible.

I was not naive about life as a Black physician in mid-20th-century Georgia. There were highly qualified Black physicians practicing in the state—especially in the major cities of Atlanta, Columbus, Savannah, and Macon—who practiced all branches of medicine. In fact, there were some who specialized in surgery and internal medicine and there was even a rare radiologist. The state of Georgia was as segregated medically as it was civically, socially, and educationally. Integration was not generally accepted in any arena. For example, there had never been a Black physician—either allopathic or osteopathic—who had qualified for membership in the Georgia State Medical Society. The reason was obvious: the color of their skin rather than their qualifications as physicians.

It was fortuitous that because of, or perhaps in spite of, this system of racial segregation and discrimination, a number of pioneering and entrepreneurial Black physicians built and operated hospitals, some of which became very creditable. This was most evident in the major cities such as Atlanta, where there were not less

A Physician in Albany

than three small Black-owned, Black-operated hospitals where Black physicians could gain privileges. In later years the city of Atlanta built an annex to Grady Hospital and named it Hughes Spalding Pavilion, which was staffed by Black physicians, practicing their skills and their art as surgeons, internists, radiologists and other branches of medicine. Other cities throughout the state of Georgia were not as fortunate; however, there were isolated cases where Black physicians would either build and operate small hospitals or there were hospitals built by the city exclusively for Black physicians.

My hometown of Americus was one of the few towns with populations less than 10,000 that had a hospital that was exclusively Black, and the only Black physician in town had full privileges. There were no Black specialists, so the White physicians in town provided all surgery, radiology, internal medicine and cardiology. These same physicians would only see Black patients in their offices from a segregated waiting room and frequently after hours.

As a very active sub-teen, I had an occasion to be admitted to the small Black hospital in Americus. While playing at building a house with chairs inside my home, I fell, striking my throat across the rail of a chair. This resulted in a fracture of my windpipe, with escape of breath from the trachea into the subcutaneous tissue. This resulted in my neck swelling periodically and rhythmically with my breathing. I was immediately taken to the local hospital for Blacks, and the only Black physician in town was called. He gained the services of a radiologist and internist who diagnosed the fractured trachea and recommended conservative treatment. I healed spontaneously without incident.

A fifty-bed hospital in Bainbridge, Georgia, was built, owned and operated by Dr. Joseph H. Griffin. Dr. Griffin had no specialty training. He practiced medicine, surgery, anesthesia, obstetrics and gynecology, cardiology, neurology, endocrinology and other branches of medicine without limitation. In my entire medical career, I have not seen a physician more versatile and more competent in more areas than Dr. Griffin. Needless to say, he was not the very best in all of these areas, yet he managed a very successful practice for more than 50 years.

~

My search for a practice site took me to many small towns in southwest Georgia where I thought that I had the best chance of success. I was greeted with much enthusiasm in most of the towns until they discovered that I was an osteopathic physician. Most didn't appear to have a particular prejudice against osteopathic physicians but simply had no knowledge of what we did. Others who had heard of osteopathic medicine wanted to have no part of it, since, with very few exceptions, the osteopathic physicians in Georgia were practicing solely manipulation, about which there was significant prejudice. Georgia law governing the practice of osteopathy specified that osteopaths could practice medicine, surgery and obstetrics "as taught." This vague law was not questioned, primarily because it was the prevailing thought that should the act be challenged, osteopaths would get full practice rights. There were those who thought the better part of wisdom was to leave the practice of osteopathy very nebulous so that it could be challenged at any time.

My step-father-in-law was urging me to locate in Atlanta, where there was the greatest concentration of Black physicians and where I had some contacts that would help in establishing a practice. Reverend Borders, my previous pastor, was pleading with me to return to Atlanta and join his son who was finishing medical school. His son, Billy, and I had gotten to know each other and Rev. Borders thought that it would be a good fit. I was not very receptive to that arrangement because Billy and I had totally different lifestyles.

I visited Albany at the invitation of Dr. Willie Joe Reese, who more than anyone else was responsible for my getting into osteopathic medicine. He offered me the opportunity to work with him or, should I choose to go it alone, he would help me get started. It was an offer too good to pass up: the opportunity to practice with another Black osteopathic physician in the southern United States, and the mentor who had helped me to become one.

I had other contacts in Albany because I on occasion would travel with my father, who had his regional insurance office there. I had met the King family, who were very well known and very well respected—influential, progressive, entrepreneurial, and enterprising. (This family was not related to Martin Luther King Jr., and, as a matter of fact, at this point, they had barely heard of him.) The Kings were unique in that they were all quite well educated and motivated toward development of business and industry. C.W. King, the father, operated two grocery stores and managed a considerable amount of rental and investment properties. Mrs. King owned and operated a women's apparel store. They had five sons: C.B., Slater, Preston, Clenon, and Allen. I was closest to C.B., who was the only Black lawyer in town (and one of very few in the entire South), and Slater, a realtor.

C.B. said to me, "Andy, Albany will be as good to you as you are to it." Enough said. I settled on Albany, stepping into a life that was totally unexpected, unplanned, only remotely related to the practice of osteopathic medicine, and that would change history.

My Practice in Albany

After a considerable amount of delay in identifying the site, I then was confronted with the myriads of problems inherent to beginning a practice. I had no money, no place in Albany to live, no equipment and no staff. So, if there's any such thing as starting at the bottom, this was it.

It was not unusual throughout the South for physicians to establish an office upstairs, usually over a drugstore. There was no Black-owned drugstore in Albany, but there was available space upstairs—over a pool hall and liquor store. These were convenient for some limited recreational activity in the pool hall and on occasion when I needed to obtain some alcoholic beverages for my visiting friends. The office was centrally located in "Harlem," a common name for Black areas in this country extending from New York to Florida and from the Carolinas to California, and the area in a community that many Blacks would seek out. The Harlem of Albany was the most popular place for Blacks to congregate in the evenings after work, and especially on weekends, when many would come to town from the rural areas. In Harlem, you could find, in addition to the liquor store and pool hall, restaurants and cafeterias, business offices that included insurance and real estate, a photographic studio, and the local newspaper. There was also a church, clothing store, barbershop, and grocery store, all within a two-block radius.

My office was well situated and very convenient to the majority of the Blacks in and around Albany, and the rent was sufficiently reasonable that I thought I could afford it. It was somewhere in the range of $50 a month, which was a fair amount for Albany in 1957. The office was large enough to have a rather comfortable waiting room that could seat as many as 15 people, a small reception area, two treatment rooms, a private office and a laboratory.

Of course, I had no equipment, so I proceeded to contact an equipment company in Atlanta. Their representative came to my office, and I described my needs, which included literally everything from furnishings and waiting room chairs, to autoclave, X-ray, needles, syringes and a lot of disposable items. The total cost was about $10,000, and I did not have the cost of postage to send in the first payment. The company representative said he would provide me with all I needed with no down payment, and I could begin making payments in three months, which I considered quite adequate to get my practice started. I was surprised that a young Black osteopath in the Deep South could buy $10,000 worth of equipment from a White-owned company in Atlanta, with no knowledge of me as a person, no knowledge of my abilities as a physician and certainly no track record on repaying such an enormous debt.

The sales representative said to me, "I have been equipping new

A Physician in Albany

doctor's offices for well over 20 years and my loss rate is only about five percent. I believe that you as a doctor, serving this community, are a good risk." At that time physicians had an excellent reputation for repaying their loans and were considered an acceptable risk.

I made my first error in practice as I began to see patients before my office was completely set up. The owner of the pool hall came to see me complaining of weakness and excessive thirst. A urine dipstick would have made the diagnosis, but I was not ready even for that simple test. Needless to say, my prescription for vitamins did not resolve his problem and he wound up at another doctor's office where the diagnosis was made. I learned my lesson early on and did not make that mistake again. There were plenty more for me to make as I built my practice and gained more and more experience. There was much more too as I discovered that patients and their diseases do not necessarily follow the medical textbooks or the classroom lectures.

Dr. Reese was most helpful to me starting out in practice including advice and tips not taught in medical school.

For example, I went with Dr. Reese on house calls where he treated everything from congestive heart failure to delivering babies. On one of the early deliveries with Dr. Reese, we found the patient, a prima gravida, to be in the early stages of labor. I performed the examination, noted she was hours away from delivery, and asked if we should come back later.

I was to learn a new definition of induced labor. Dr. Reese, much to my amazement, said, "We will not be here for several hours. We will have this baby now." He said, "Look in my bag and you will find a vial of Pituitrin and one of Pitocin. Give her both." That is where the practical side of practice negated the scientific medicine that I had been taught.

I said, "Should I give her a minimum or a drop of each in a liter of intravenous infusion and at ten drops per minute?"

He said, "No, give her both vials, intramuscularly, and get ready to deliver the baby." I stood in shock but bowed to his years of experience and gave her what he asked.

In a very few minutes and after a few very forceful contractions, we had a baby. I learned a valuable lesson that contradicted much of what I learned in medical school. The baby arrived,

gave a healthy cry, and the mother was soon relieved and happy. I was the one who had to recover from the new experience.

It was as though the people in and around Albany had anticipated my coming. Almost from the first day I had an office full of patients—on some days as many as 100. This was indicative of the need for more physicians in the area who would listen, diagnose and attend carefully to the needs of Black patients. The practice of medicine as I experienced it when I first went to Albany, was anything other than current, personal, sacred or private. In the office of some of the White allopathic physicians who would accept Black patients, the patients were seen in groups, perhaps as many as five, after hours and in a back waiting room. The patients would sit around in a semicircle as the physician, sitting in his chair, not having touched the patient for an examination, would simply ask about the symptoms.

"What's wrong with you, boy?"

The answer may come, "Doctor, my ankles and legs are swelling and I'm short of breath."

"And you, auntie, what's wrong with you?"

"I get up through the night to go to the bathroom and my urine is thick like syrup and I'm rapidly losing weight."

"All right," the doctor would say, "you, boy, come and get a shot every week." This would usually be Mercuhydrin, a mercurial diuretic, very toxic to kidneys.

"And for you, auntie, you get a low-sugar diet and take these pills." The pills would usually be an oral hypoglycemic agent that was only recently being introduced into the market, but rapidly taking the place of insulin, which was more difficult to manage.

This was not an uncommon practice on Black patients in the 1950s. Yet this is not intended to indict all the White physicians, as

A Physician in Albany

there were some who were trapped in a society that demanded the segregation of the races, who were yet committed to the principles of the good practice of medicine, and that would not permit them to abandon all standards of practice, even on Blacks.

I took care of all their ailments and diseases--including hypertension, diabetes, congestive heart failure, and obstetrics and gynecology. I even would care for simple fractures and I did minor surgery in my office. By any and all definitions, my practice was a complete success. I was only limited by the lack of hospital privileges.

There was but one hospital in the city of Albany: Phoebe Putney Hospital. While there had been other Black physicians in Albany, none had ever been granted hospital privileges. Jake Shirley, MD, became a very close friend and frequently covered me in my practice, but could never gain hospital privileges at Phoebe Putney because he was not a member of the Georgia State Medical Society, which had as a condition of joining being something other than Black. Dr. Reese was the only other Black physician in Albany and of course he was denied because of his color, lack of membership in the Georgia State Medical Society, and moreover, he was an osteopathic physician.

I did not go through the formal process of applying for hospital privileges. I merely began sending patients to the hospital, and proceeded to go there and write orders, which were promptly carried out. This continued for several weeks until someone complained. I was summoned by the hospital administrator and I accepted the invitation to meet with him.

He asked, "Are you a member of the Georgia State Medical Society?" Of course, he knew the answer because there had never been a Black member accepted for membership. He knew all of the answers that he could use to deny me hospital privileges, yet he went through the motions. But by the time my non-application had been rejected, there were a few other staff physicians who had begun to see some of the patients whom I had referred for specialty care—primarily orthopedics, internal medicine, or cardiology. These physicians I remember specifically because they are the ones who, after learning of my denial of hospital privileges, either called or sent messages that they would continue to accept my patients in consultation as they felt as though my quality and style of practice was as good as others on the staff of Phoebe Putney.

I also made house calls. On one particular night I went to visit a patient who had been sick for several weeks and had been to see doctors during the daytime who would not visit him at night. I found this to be a very common practice—one that I came to deplore. There were patients who would accept my care at night because I made house calls, but during the day they would go to see the White doctor downtown. After a few such experiences, I became indignant and in this particular case I said to the family of the patient, "If I'm not good enough to treat him during the day when I'm in my office, I'm not good enough to come and treat him at night."

I made a diagnosis of pancreatitis without benefit of any laboratory tests. I referred the patient to Phoebe Putney where he was examined in the emergency room and was admitted. The next day the attending physician called to say, "That was a hell of a diagnosis to be made without benefit of any laboratory tests or X-rays." I replied, "Well, now you know the difference between MDs and DOs."

From that point on, I began to get the respect of a number of the White doctors on staff, who were willing to accept my patients on referral but yet reluctant to send me a consultation report. Out of frustration I began to refer patients not to Phoebe Putney but to more distant sites such as Americus, my hometown, about 40 miles away, but the next closest hospital. Again, my patients were well received by the specialist, and I would even get some consultation reports. I continued this referral pattern as long as there were patients willing to travel the distance.

After being in practice for a couple of years, I elected to expand my office facility as I found it most inconvenient and too time-consuming to make house calls to deliver babies at home. Some of the at-home deliveries were quite traumatic for me, the mother and the baby. I frequently made house calls in homes that did not have

A Physician in Albany

electricity or running water, central heat or air conditioning. On occasion a patient in labor would be placed across the bed sideways with two straight chairs to hold the feet and legs. I would drive my automobile up to the window and shine the automobile lights through the window so that I could see as I delivered the baby. It is amazing what you discover you can do out of necessity—things that were never taught in medical school or you will never read in a medical textbook. Yet it's what many rural physicians still do today.

I soon came to the conclusion that if I were to continue with this volume in my practice, it would be necessary to expand my in-office hours and have them come there so that I could see more patients. I therefore extended my office sufficiently to accommodate two hospital beds. I also found it necessary to expand my staff. From the beginning I had a front-office person and a back-office person who were cross trained. I found it necessary to hire a third person primarily to care for the obstetrical patients and the minor surgical patients that I treated at the office.

A.C. Searles, the local newspaper editor and a good friend, was also the girls' basketball coach and the business instructor at the local high school. I asked for a recommendation for a receptionist and bookkeeper. He referred one of his recent high school graduates who could not afford to go off to college and who had begun working as a maid in one of the downtown stores. Based on his recommendation, I invited her in for an interview. I was impressed with her basic knowledge and ability to be a fast learner, so we then began to discuss salaries. It seemed as though several hours passed as we were negotiating between $25 and $30 per week for her services. Yes, I said between $25 and $30 a week. Thirty dollars was on the high end of a salary for a recent high school graduate in Albany.

I look back on that negotiation session and laugh, because by the time I closed my practice in Albany she was making $300 a week and was worth much more. She was an astute observer and a quick learner, mixed with personality skills and talent far beyond her educational years. She literally could run my practice for weeks without me, taking care of regular blood pressure and blood sugar checks and routine prenatal examinations. She was sufficiently knowledgeable and skilled to recognize when there was a problem and could refer the patient to either Dr. Reese or Dr. Shirley, who willingly accepted my patients while I was out of town. Ms. Mary Perry was her name. She was dependable, honest and smart and one of the best hires I ever made.

A Member of the Albany Community

As soon as I secured an office and equipment, I proceeded to search for a house. Joe Malone was a name well-known throughout Albany, for he was a very wealthy Black businessman who owned multiple properties. His home base was in Harlem where he sold a variety of things, which included tobacco products, soft drinks, candy, crackers, etc. He was noted for having some of the finest cigars; however, they were always one, two, or three or more days old because he would buy the leftovers from sales at the downtown hotel. The hotel would not sell stale cigars to its customers; Malone was known to buy the stale cigars to sell to his customers, who were not as sophisticated in their taste.

I contacted Malone and he proceeded to show me properties that he had for sale, and, incidentally, he said, he would also finance the sale. We found a small house of four rooms in the Washington Heights subdivision of Albany. I used the word "subdivision" rather loosely. It was a section just outside of town in the midst of a pine forest where a few trees had been removed to make room for houses to be built. There were no paved roads, although we had electricity, and there was no sewage system, so we depended on septic tanks to dispose of waste. But we were fortunate to have lights, water, and a roof over our heads. Home air conditioning was yet to be made available in Albany other than businesses and the very wealthy. Our first home cost $6,000 (that of course we did not have) but Malone was willing to accept a small down payment and monthly payments thereafter.

We moved in and immediately gained friends in the neighborhood. Jake Shirley was the only Black M.D. in town who frequently covered my practice while I was in jail or traveling to events. His wife, Modesque, was more of a community activist than Jake. Together they made quite a contrast in personalities.

Norma, Modesque Shirley, Cora Powell, Marian King, Alma Chatman, Anna Meeks, and other women in our subdivision became known as "agitators" and were a constant thorn in the side of the city council with their many petitions to improve the neighborhood. The Council reluctantly capitulated on several of the petitions more out of self-defense than a sincere willingness to improve living conditions for Blacks. The results of their efforts were apparent in neighborhood parks and recreation equipment.

These same women played a vital role in the Albany Movement. They were at every mass rally, led marches and sit-ins, directed the carpool and hosted hundreds of outsiders that came to join in the movement.

All of our children were in the best schools that Albany had to offer, including the Laboratory Training School for Albany State College. This school had some outstanding teachers that were committed to providing the very best, well-rounded education for the select few Black children that could qualify for admission. The qualifications were as much economic status and position in society as academic achievement.

Odessa Hamilton and Dobinian Clark were among the most notable and memorable of the teachers. This school, Hazard Training School, reinforced the lessons we had taught our children, such as how to bank and save and shop, how to develop good social skills,

A Member of the Albany Community

and how to practice good manners and ethics. The lessons that they learned at Hazard prepared them for further education and have served them well in their adult lives. This was indeed one of the finest schools we had ever seen.

Gaining some economic success and financial security that I had not previously experienced, I was faced with a welcome problem—that of having some excess money. Norma and I had been married most of our adult lives and at no time previously did we have to deal with an amount of money that was not already overcommitted to accumulated debt.

My step-father-in-law, while very erratic, somewhat eccentric and always unpredictable, managed to associate with some of the most successful and highly respected business people in Atlanta. He was not only a well-known minister, but he also held prestigious positions in the National Baptist Convention and was editor of the Georgia State Baptist Publications.

He was well-known for his fiery temper and even more for his fiery verbal outbursts. Roland Smith took great pride and enormous satisfaction in challenging anyone on any subject, in any forum at any time. His unique manner was manifest in all of the organizations with which he was affiliated, and they were many. Roland, who also served on the SCLC board of directors, was selected to serve on the board of the nation's oldest Black bank, Citizens Trust Company of Atlanta. He served on the bank board with Martin Luther King Sr., who became one of his best and closest friends. You certainly could not tell how close these two were should you judge by the frequent personal confrontations, in or out of formal business meetings. King, Sr. and Roland were both strong of will and determination and they rarely ever agreed on anything. Yet, they found common ground in the ministry and in banking.

The Citizens Bank's board was composed of the leading Black businessmen of Atlanta. Yes, men, I again said. Women were excluded from the banking business at that time. On the board were such notable dignitaries as J.L. Milton, C.R. Yates, William Calloway,

Harry Richardson, J.B. Blayton and Herman Russell among others—all successful businessmen.

Roland would more often than not disrupt the board meetings with his outbursts, with or without just cause. He did not need a reason to explode with a verbal attack, just an opportunity. When there was no opportunity, he had a way of making one.

Roland's deportment did not improve in the board meetings of the SCLC. This board was dominated by preachers, all of whom were respected leaders within their own domain, their pulpits. These preachers all had strong opinions that they did not hesitate to express, and they were almost never wrong, at least in their own minds. This was fertile ground for Roland. These board meetings were always very lively and often confrontational, bordering on violence that never happened but was always anticipated. Roland, being of small stature, weighing barely 125 pounds and stretching to about 5-foot-5, knew just how far to go and how hard to push in his challenges. He was not one to take defeat lightly and always would have the last word, even if no one was left to hear it.

Because of Roland's propensity to disrupt meetings, Dr. King was asked why he kept Roland on his board. His response was, "Roland kept everyone honest, for he would never allow anything to be swept under the rug, ignored or glossed over." King considered this a valuable asset in his organization. Roland was a "take no prisoners" type of board member.

I valued Roland's advice, although I rarely followed it. Nonetheless, I shall be forever grateful for the advice he gave me about the management of my excess money. His advice was to get it out of Albany and establish a banking relationship at Citizens Trust Bank. I followed that wisdom, and it led to my getting to know the Black leaders of Atlanta.

He further advised me to purchase stock in the bank. Roland at the time was one of their large stockholders, and desired for a member of his family also to share in the success or failure of this venture that was yet rare in Black America. I was technically not a

A Member of the Albany Community

member of Roland's family except by marriage to his stepdaughter. But Roland had no other family except for a sister, with whom he was not very close. He had no children of his own, so if he were to leave a legacy, I was about as close as one would get. I accepted the role, and his advice.

I continued to buy CTB stock for many years until I became one of the major stockholders and eventually a member of the board of directors, a position that I held for 24 years. The financial rewards were minimal, but I found great satisfaction in being a part of an ongoing Black-owned financial institution that served many Black people who would not otherwise have had access to needed capital.

As a member of the CTB board I had the opportunity to learn from L.D. Milton, the bank president, who was a brilliant banker, successful operator of a drugstore, and property owner.

J.B. Blayton was the first Black certified public accountant in Georgia and founder of the first Black-owned and operated radio station. This was the station that gave me my first break in radio broadcasting. Blayton also owned a business school that trained hundreds of Blacks in business and accounting. He was a role model for countless aspiring businesspeople.

Herman Russell, reputedly the most successful Black contractor and builder in America, owned many corporations, providing not only construction, but also property management and airport concessions in cities across the United States. Herman and I became good friends and occasionally traveled together, seeking out business opportunities and attending banking conventions. Herman is a most interesting figure, who literally took a small fledging plastering company to a multi-million-dollar empire. With all of his success and enormous wealth, he remained unpretentious and unassuming. His wonderful wife, Otellia, often referred to him as "cheap," mostly because he was frugal when it came to luxuries. Notwithstanding this characterization by his wife, Herman was generous with his time and money in worthwhile causes and when he entertained, he did it in a very lavish style.

Johnnie Clark, a brilliant woman, was a tremendous asset to the bank board because of her background in business and finance. Johnnie, for many years, was a teacher in the Atlanta University system. She was highly regarded as an educator and could have been a banker should she had chosen to do so. It was Johnnie who stabilized the bank during the periods between presidents.

Juanita Sellers Stone was a member of the Sellers family who operated several funeral homes in and around Atlanta. She was an asset to the bank because of her family identity and involvement in many community activities. The Sellers were highly regarded for the successful businesses that they operated.

James Paschal was well known for his restaurant business. He and his brother also owned and operated airport concessions, a hotel, and a nightclub. In his own quiet and unpretentious way, he amassed considerable wealth and fame as a very enterprising businessman.

William Calloway, a distant relative of the world-renowned Cab Calloway, was a very active CTB board member. Bill had a distinguished career as an educator and realtor. He had the added distinction of being one of my wife's teachers in high school. That would give you some idea of his age at the time.

R.K. Siegal was one of very few non-African Americans selected for CTB board. Siegal had a strong background in engineering and construction and had come from one of the most successful engineering companies in the world. With his knowledge and wit, he brought another dimension to the bank board. He often challenged the culture of the bank when it hampered its growth. There were those on the bank board that did not take very kindly to this characterization from an outsider, yet we had to concede that there was a problem that needed to be fixed. We devoted much attention to fixing that culture.

Tom Bolden was the other non-African American on the bank board. Tom had a lifetime of experience gathered from years with another major bank. His expertise and advice were invaluable, and he gave both freely. Tom had lived a somewhat sheltered life, with

A Member of the Albany Community

limited exposure to the Black community. He sought to remedy that by getting to know many of us on a personal basis. I came to respect him for his sensitivity and commitment to do the right thing. Tom was the first to invite me to one of the most prestigious private clubs in Atlanta. This was a small gesture, yet symbolic of a bigger thing—acceptance on a personal and business level.

My service on the CTB board of directors spanned nearly two and a half decades. I saw the bank go through many changes. There were the ups and downs of the market reflected in our profits and there were periods of failed investment programs. I worked with four presidents and one acting president during the 24 years that I was there.

As chairman of the Strategic Planning Committee, I was part of projecting goals that could not be realistically attained. This was not due to lack of banking skills and knowledge but rather an inability to access the necessary markets to become a major bank. Black banks at that time could only rise so high before bumping into that economic ceiling. No Black bank was ever able to reach the billion-dollar threshold that opened doors to major, highly profitable investments. After that, Black banks could compete in the world markets.

I consider my service on the CTB board well spent years. My only regret is that I did not stay to see my dreams of CTB becoming a major bank come true.

Harlem Cut-Rate Drugs

Many of my patients were schoolteachers, businesspeople, and other professionals who could afford better health care than they were receiving at the hands of most of the White doctors practicing in the Albany area. Female patients, when they had to receive a prescription, were often treated with less than appropriately courteous treatment. In contrast, it was customary in my practice to write the patient's name preceded by a title. A patient I'll call "Mrs. James" went to the drugstore to have a prescription filled, and she anticipated that on the bottle her name would appear just as it had on the prescription: "Mrs. Thelma James." When she received the prescription she noted "Mrs." was missing, whereupon she asked the pharmacist, "Is this the way my doctor wrote the prescription?"

He said, "No, Thelma, but it has the right medicine in it."

She gave the prescription bottle back to the pharmacist and said, "I would like for my name on the prescription bottle to read the same as the prescription as written by my doctor."

The pharmacist refused. She returned to my office and I referred her to another pharmacist. It came to my attention that my patients should have a choice of pharmacist, and certainly one who would extend to them the courtesies and dignities that they deserved. I called together a number of business people, including a dentist, physician, photographer, and two of the King brothers, and we decided to build a drugstore in Harlem. "Harlem Cut-Rate Drugs" would be owned and operated by Blacks and for Blacks. We pooled our resources, renovated a building in Harlem, and in a few short months we were open for business. This venture was very successful, and Black patients could shop for their drugs, toiletry items, beauty aids and other products customarily found in other drugstores, but for the first time in an atmosphere of dignity and respect.

Upon completion of renovations of the building for the new drugstore, we initiated a nationwide search for a Black pharmacist. These were few and far between. We were drawn to Hiram Sanders, whom I remembered as a schoolmate at Fort Valley State College. He was now a graduate-registered pharmacist available for employment. Hiram was torn between Atlanta and his hometown of Thomasville, Georgia, but we convinced him that he had a very bright future in Albany. We assured him that at some point, he could become the sole owner and, in fact, that he would be given stock in the drugstore from the beginning. He accepted the offer and became the first Black pharmacist in Albany.

Hiram was somewhat bashful and retiring, and although in his early thirties, he had never been married, nor had he seriously considered it. Notwithstanding his casual demeanor, Hiram was a very competent pharmacist. He was not aggressive, however, always looking for deals, discounts or lower prices.

Kianmo Builders: A Venture into Real Estate

Slater King became my business partner. He had real-estate knowledge, I had some capital, and we both knew a competent builder. We formed the Kianmo Builders Corporation for King, Anderson, and Morris. Kianmo built houses in the Albany area, some for sale and some for rent. This proved to be a successful venture in that the houses were easily marketable, and we sold them as fast as we erected them. While the rental units were always occupied, I learned early on that real estate was not for me. I had little interest in building and selling properties, and certainly less interest in managing them, so I eventually sold most of the rental property.

The Albany Movement
1961–1963

By any standard of measure for a Black doctor in the heart of the deep, segregated South, my work in Albany was a success. I always had an abundance of loyal patients, a good staff, and a satisfying and rewarding practice with a comfortable income. I soon became involved in local civic and social organizations that included the NAACP (National Association for the Advancement of Colored People), Urban League and the Criterion Club. Of these, the Criterion Club was the club of the elite, and its members were business, educational, and professional men (this was an all-male club at the time).

The NAACP and Urban League were well organized but had little impact on the segregation, discrimination, and denial of voters' rights in Albany. All of the recognized Black leaders in town belonged to one or more of these organizations. We met regularly and discussed the problems but felt helpless to do much about them.

William G Anderson, DO, FACOS

SNCC: The First Impetus for Change

That changed when, in September 1961, the Student Nonviolent Coordinating Committee (SNCC), led by field officers Charles Sherrod and Cordell Reagon, arrived in Terrell County to begin voter registration drives, aggressively recruiting Blacks to attempt to register to vote. Of course, all of their efforts were rebuffed as the city clerk always managed to find a way to deny the right to register. Impossible literacy tests, excessively long "lunch breaks," and sporadic hours for opening the registration office served to dissuade and discourage the would-be voters.

The SNCC was led by dedicated civil rights workers who were effective because they were committed to the struggle and less concerned for worldly goods, of which they had little to none. These brave students could afford to be daring to the point of recklessness, for they had little if anything to lose, except some time in jail or perhaps a life here and there. They considered those risks as the cost of advancing the Civil Rights Movement. SNCC and the Congress of Racial Equality (CORE), as other newly organized civil rights organizations, had received their motivation from the successful Montgomery bus boycott led by that young preacher from Dexter Avenue Baptist Church, Martin Luther King Jr. Other civil rights organizations, such as NAACP and the Urban League, had been around for many years.

Charles Jones, Charles Sherrod, Diane Nash, James Foreman and other young men and women formed the nucleus of SNCC in Albany. I do not know how they came to our city, but they were the undisputed spark of the Albany Movement. They recruited high school kids, trained them in nonviolent protest, and involved them in demonstrations, which started with simple picketing downtown—picketing that was consistent with the law. However, the city would not issue a permit to demonstrate, and the small gatherings led to marches on City Hall. These efforts led to arrests—first small groups of high school children then larger and larger groups of all ages. This

The Albany Movement

series of demonstrations continued for several months and was rapidly gaining momentum and getting the attention of the local government and all social and civic organizations in town.

(left to right): Slater King, vice president of the Albany Movement, and SNCC leaders Charles Jones and James Foreman confronted barriers to voter registration.

Serendipity, ICC, and the Formation of the Albany Movement

An opportune but unplanned impetus for these students was offered by a ruling by the Interstate Commerce Commission (ICC) requiring the desegregation of interstate transportation facilities, which became law on November 1, 1961. That very day, students sat in at the Trailways bus station in Albany to test the new law.

We quickly formed a loose organization to begin to coordinate the activities of what would become the Albany Movement. My wife, Norma, drafted some of our neighbors and other women in Albany to test the ICC ruling and to participate in other movement activities. Anna Meeks and Cora Powell, wives of career servicemen, were among the first to be drafted. Anna served as the secretary, and Cora used her musical talents as a singer and pianist to encourage and motivate those who attended the mass rallies. Among the others who joined in the activities were Marian King, wife of Slater, who became the movement vice president, and Ruth Hunter, wife of an Albany State College faculty member. These courageous women placed their security and futures in jeopardy, as there was the continuous threat of reprisals with loss of jobs, mortgages, and credit for those who participated in the movement activities.

Inspired by our youth, all of the then-known Civil Rights organizations came together at this point for a common cause: to put an end to segregation in Albany—a movement that would soon envelop the entire nation. The organizational meeting took place late at night on November 17, 1961, at the home of Ed Hamilton, a local dentist who for many years had been a community activist. Ed was highly respected as a man of integrity and was totally dedicated to his hometown.

With the sole exception of the NAACP, every civil rights group in Albany, the old and the new, had representatives at the meeting. There were already scores of demonstrators in jail as a result of our picketing and from the arrest of the students testing the ICC ruling. There was much discussion but, surprisingly, little disagreement on what course of action we should take. All agreed that we should organize as a single group and elect a single leader with support officers.

We then needed a name. Needless to say, each of the organizations represented would have been pleased to take the leadership and have the movement under its banner. It was generally appreciated that such organizations needed to be identified and widely publicized in order to gain and maintain support. Fundraising was vitally necessary for any of the civil rights groups.

Many of us insisted on avoiding an identity with a single organization. I am certain that there was a bit of hesitation and reluctance on the part of some to accept a neutral name, but the majority was in total support of the idea. It was thought that a generic name would prevent any one organization from taking credit for the movement, an act that might alienate the others. After a considerable amount of

The Albany Movement

discussion, someone finally said, "Why not just call it The Albany Movement?" It immediately stuck.

Our next task was to select a president and a slate of officers. This proved, surprisingly, to be a relatively easy task, for they looked for someone with no Albany "baggage," one who had not antagonized too many people, and one who had a good reputation for honesty and integrity. And, by the way, he or she also had to be willing to serve. I was chosen to be president, not because of any expertise that I had in civil rights, but because I was relatively new in town and had not as yet managed to make many enemies. It was also considered that, as a practicing physician with few, if any, White patients, I was pretty much immune to economic sanctions that would very likely be imposed on the leaders of the movement.

Slater King, the brother of C.B. King and an enterprising and successful businessman, was selected as the vice president. Slater and I worked hand in hand, leading the movement, planning the strategy, and continuing to motivate the people that joined us. With his wife, Marian, they were active participants and willing demonstrators who frequented the jails of southwest Georgia at least as much as I did.

Among the Albany Black community's leadership were (left to right) Marian King, Thomas Chatmon, and Slater King.

William G Anderson, DO, FACOS

Albany's Cast of Characters

Behind the headlines that would come to describe the Albany Movement was a remarkable array of people and organizations, working in cooperation to finance, feed, transport, shelter, support, and communicate all of the activities that were necessary to create significant social change.

Without the cooperation of the Black churches and their ministers, neither the Albany Movement nor other Civil Rights Movements in America would have been possible. We are deeply indebted to the ministers of Albany for opening up their churches for the mass rallies and for business meetings. This was not without risk, as most of the pastors had other jobs since the churches could not afford a sufficient salary to support the minister and his family. In fact, some ministers were threatened with the loss of their jobs, or loss of mortgages on their churches, or other forms of reprisal for their participation in the Civil Rights Movement.

(Left to right) The Revs. Willie Boyd, Martin Luther King, and Vincent Harding, Rose Harding, the Revs. Wyatt Tee Walker and Ben Gay, and me (Dr. Anderson).

The first rallies were held at Shiloh Baptist Church, pastored by The Rev. William Boyd, and Mount Zion Baptist Church, pastored by

The Albany Movement

The Rev. E. James Grant. These churches were directly across the street from each other and became the headquarters for the mass meetings. These ministers were fearless. Reverend Grant was also the principal of a high school in Baker County, one of the most notoriously racist counties in Georgia. I will always admire and respect the Rev. Grant for opening up his church to The Albany Movement, knowing full well that his job and security in Baker County were threatened every day.

Mount Zion Church was probably nearly 100 years old and deteriorating, with the threat of condemnation when the movement started. Yet it was sufficiently structurally sound to permit the mass meetings to occur. I joined Mt. Zion when I first moved to Albany because of my background in the Baptist Church, but also because several of my friends were members there, including the King family and the Hamilton family. Ed and Odessa Hamilton were very close friends of ours, and we had known them for many years. They were not only community activists, but were also highly respected as leaders in the church and in social and civic affairs.

Black churches were invaluable to the movement, and clergy took significant risk in marching. (Left to right) The Revs. E.J. Grant, Paul Davenport, Westley Lowe, L.W. Shite, and Roland Mosely.

The members of Mt. Zion were not noted for being very good stewards of their church, and this was true even of my friend Ed Hamilton. Norma and I started a trend of giving in Mt. Zion that was unheard of. We gave as much as $40 a month, which of course, was not tithing, but was far in excess of other members of the church. Hamilton indicated that he was very generous with his church in that he gave $10 every month, with the exception of June, July, and August, which were vacation months, when he did not give at all. We are proud of the fact that we motivated not only Ed Hamilton but others to increase their giving in support of Mt. Zion, which later proved to be so pivotal to the Albany Movement.

There were many other ministers in the Albany community who opened their churches and raised funds in support of the movement. I am not aware of a single Black congregation without regard to denomination that refused to assist, either by making its building available or by raising funds. The Rev. Ben Gay, who pastored Bethel AME Church, the Rev. Rozwell Smith, pastor of Third Kiokee Baptist church, and the pastors of Friendship and Mt. Olive churches, and others throughout the area, were willing supporters and participants in the Albany Movement.

The Rev. Joe Smith, a young, up-and-coming preacher and son of the Rev. Rozwell Smith, coordinated the carpool and was tireless, working long hours from sun up until well into the night to make certain that transportation needs were met. Without the carpool, many of the Blacks who depended on employment in White neighborhoods would have been severely hurt. Many others volunteered their automobiles, and some fuel was provided by Odum's Gulf and other Black-owned gas stations.

As noted, we lived in a Black subdivision just outside of Albany called Washington Heights. Several of the women who lived in the subdivision had formed an organization to improve the conditions in the neighborhood. My wife, Norma, along with Mrs. Powell, Chatmon, Meeks, and King, formed the Washington Heights Improvement Association, which spearheaded the move to improve

The Albany Movement

playgrounds, roads, and life in the subdivision. This same group became very active in the Albany Movement and attended the rallies, drove in the carpools, and opened their homes to civil rights workers who came to join us from the outside.

Because of the many threats that my family and I received during the height of the movement, we often found it necessary to sleep away from home. John and Richardene Chadwell frequently kept our children. She was a public school teacher, and he was the chairman of the department of music at Albany State College. Both placed their jobs in jeopardy by supporting the movement. Without the comfort and support afforded to us by the Chadwells in overseeing our children, we would not have been able to continue.

On the occasions when Norma was in jail, and I was out, I found refuge in the home of Willie Odum, who operated the Gulf gas station. He was a strong supporter of the Albany Movement and opened up his home for me, providing safety and security for me at no little risk to himself.

A.C. Searles was editor of the local Black newspaper, a high school teacher, and girls' basketball coach. Mr. Searles never missed a meeting and was a most reliable source of information on the movement activities. As a public school teacher, he ran the risk of losing his job for providing any support or encouragement to the demonstrators. He willingly took that risk and did it every day.

Schoolteachers from various elementary and high schools actively participated in the movement activities. Most visible were teachers from Monroe and Madison High, and to a lesser extent, there was participation from teachers and faculty of Albany State College. It is unfortunate that the president of Albany State College formally prohibited faculty, staff, and students from participating in the Albany Movement activities. Yet, notwithstanding this announced prohibition, many students, some teachers, and some administrators actively participated or were otherwise supportive.

For example, Wilhelmina Dye Hall, a local high school teacher, was present at every mass rally and functioned as a secretary to the

William G Anderson, DO, FACOS

Albany Movement on frequent occasions. Her husband Jack and his father were constantly present at all the movement activities, including the major marches. Daddy Hall, who was in his eighties, was among the first to get up early in the morning and dressed warmly prepared to meet others at Shiloh church for a march to jail. When asked, "What are you doing?"

He responded, "I am marching for my freedom."

Irene Wright was a member of the faculty of Albany State College and wife of an officer in the Air Force. Irene early on defended SNCC and, in fact, helped to recruit a number of students from Albany State College for the movement. Many meetings were held in her home, and she frequently attended the mass rallies. Her husband was cautioned that his participation might jeopardize his position in the military.

No account of the Albany Movement would be complete without a mention of two of the most dedicated, committed, and courageous civil rights activists, W.W. Law and C.K. Steele. By 1960, Law was already a legend in civil rights activity. Unlike many of the other leaders of the Civil Rights Movement, he was a postman, not a preacher. He led demonstrations in Savannah, Georgia, testing the laws of segregation and discrimination for several years before the Albany Movement. His motivation and inspiration came from the Montgomery bus boycott.

C.K. Steele was from Tallahassee, Florida, and was well known in that capital city as a civil rights activist. Both of these civil rights pioneers came to Albany at the beginning of the movement and offered their services, including participation in strategy sessions, in picketing and marches.

Every attempt was made to dissuade, discourage and intimidate the Negroes who participated by attending the nightly mass meetings or joining the marchers or the picketers, including acts of violence, most notably the burning of several churches in and around Albany. Churches were fire-bombed in Dougherty, Lee, and Baker Counties. This series of church bombings prompted a visit by baseball legend

The Albany Movement

Jackie Robinson, one of the high points in the Albany Movement. He stayed at our home, which was the headquarters for the movement, and visited the rubble that had once housed active congregations. Before he left, Robinson made a commitment to help raise money to rebuild all of the bombed-out churches. His visit was followed by more monetary contributions to the Albany Movement.

There seemingly was a steady stream of interested people from all walks of life who were eager to participate in the Albany Movement. Our home was filled with people of all races and religions. Rabbi Curt Flasher was one who stayed for several weeks during the height of the demonstrations. While he was a welcomed guest, his orthodox dietary requirements placed an extra burden on my wife, who found it difficult to keep kosher foods available.

Touring smoldering ashes of a Black church with (left to right) baseball legend Jackie Robinson, and The Rev. W.T. Walker.

Mrs. Lucille Walker, a long-time Albany resident, had been our housekeeper prior to the movement, practically moved in during the height of the demonstrations. She became the cook not only for our family but also for the scores of people who found their way to our home. Mrs. Walker soon learned the favorite meals of both Dr. King and Rev. Abernathy; Dr. King was especially fond of her potato pies, while Rev. Abernathy was more apt to go for the greens and cornbread. King was so impressed with Mrs. Walker's cooking that he took her back to Atlanta with him after the Albany Movement was over, and she became his live-in cook.

To characterize all the Whites in Albany as being rabid racists would be unfair. There were some whom I felt were trapped in this society and bound by the laws that imposed racial segregation. Ironically, most notable among those who were amenable to change were Mayor Asa Kelley and Police Chief Laurie Pritchett. I cannot say the same for members of the City Council, or for many of the other city fathers. Sheriff James Campbell was among those most resistant to any change in Albany, and one who never embraced the nonviolent approach to counteracting civil rights demonstrations. One time, he viciously struck our lawyer, C.B. King, when C.B. attempted to meet with one of the demonstrators in jail. This sheriff never relented in his efforts to squash the civil rights movement.

It was early in the demonstrations that Chief Pritchett, noting that I had been arrested, directed the policeman to escort me to his office. I was impressed with his sincerity and sensitivity. It was apparent that his strong religious background, his personal moral convictions, and his professionalism were being tested by the segregation rules he was required to enforce. The chief, in his freshly starched uniform, stood toe-to-toe with me, and in a very deliberate manner, he placed his hand over his heart and said, "Dr. Anderson, by all of this marching and demonstration, do you think this is the way to make people like you?"

I responded, "Chief, you will never know whether or not you can like me so long as laws, traditions, and customs keep us apart."

It is ironic that Chief Pritchett and I became the very best of friends after the movement was over. During the filming of the documentary *Eyes on the Prize*, we met for the first time as equals and as newfound friends. We maintained contact by visiting, letter-writing and always greetings for the religious holiday observances.

While the spark for the Albany Movement was the youth, primarily SNCC, who recruited many of the high school and college

The Albany Movement

students, it rapidly expanded to include Blacks of all ages, from all walks of life, and from all occupations and professions. Many came to the regular nightly mass rallies that counted in the hundreds to thousands; others prepared food for those who had come to town in support of the movement. Still others provided housing and transportation. These were important because there were no hotel accommodations and very limited cafeteria facilities for out-of-towners.

Harlem was the center of activity for Blacks in the Albany area, but another popular site was on the outskirts of town. "Cabins in the Pines" included a small motel, several cabins, and two eating establishments. It was a unique property owned by Bo Riggins, who had a keen sense of business and designed his services to accommodate a wide variety of people. At the front of the property was an upscale restaurant and entertainment facility, where schoolteachers, professionals, and visiting dignitaries could eat in comfort. He also had a second restaurant, set further back, where you could be comfortable in overalls, sweatshirts, with or without shoes—drinking beer while munching on pigs' feet, neck bones, and pork skins. The small motel and the multiple cabins served a variety of needs, including a place for visitors who elected not to stay in the private homes of other Blacks in town.

Koinonia Farm had been started by The Rev. Clarence Jordan, author of the famous *Cotton Patch Gospels*, near Americus. Koinonia Farm was integrated from the beginning and operated much like a commune. The residents shared everything and supported each other. They helped to build each other's homes. They worshipped together. They ate together and they lived together, and they attended the mass rallies and demonstrations in Albany together. They were as much a part of the Albany Movement as any of the people who lived in Albany proper.

On occasion, we would visit the farm, where you would find the finest example of integration and cooperation in an atmosphere of peace, love and brotherhood of any place I have ever witnessed. There were no racial, class, or ethnic restrictions on those living or visiting. But the people of Koinonia were also isolated from nearby Americus. Many merchants refused to sell them food, machinery, and other products; they were denied access to credit. In fact, Koinonia Farm was the object of many violent attacks, including drive-by shootings, burning of homes, and general threats and intimidation against the people who would venture into Americus and other surrounding towns.

Notwithstanding all of this, the people of Koinonia were dedicated and committed to the principles of brotherhood, a philosophy that was expounded constantly by Rev. Clarence Jordan. Ultimately, they became national leaders in community initiatives, and the founders of Habitat for Humanity International.

The Battle Is Joined

On November 22, 1961, five Black students, testing the desegregation ruling of the Interstate Commerce Commission, were arrested for sitting in the "Whites-only" section of the Trailways bus station in Albany. These brave youth galvanized the Black community of the city, and on November 25, we called the Albany Movement into action at our first mass meeting at Mt. Zion Baptist Church. Hundreds attended. The students were tried on November 27, and the Black community marched in protest.

On December 10th, an integrated group of nine Freedom Riders arrived in Albany by train. It was generally known that the Freedom Riders were testing the desegregation ruling of the Interstate Commerce Commission, but no one knew or could have anticipated that Albany was on their itinerary. The Freedom Riders were dedicated men and women from all walks of life and from varied organizations, including members of NAACP, SNCC, CORE, and the Urban League.

When the Freedom Riders came to town, Albany was already in the throes of the first real test of Jim Crow laws. Without hesitation, the police, citing a disturbance of the peace, arrested all the Freedom Riders as they attempted to utilize the Whites-only waiting room and restroom facilities in the train station. News of these arrests spread rapidly across Georgia and the rest of the United States. Overnight, Albany became the focal point of the Civil Rights Movement in America.

I certainly had anticipated there would be many arrests in Albany, but I had assumed that they would be nonviolent and consistent with the practice that had been established by Martin Luther King Jr. in Montgomery some five years earlier. One morning at my breakfast table, I was trying to explain to my children that before this was over, it was very likely that I would be arrested. But they were to understand that I was not going to jail because I was a criminal or a bad person or had done anything that was injurious to someone. The conversation was necessary because we had all been brought up to believe that the only people who go to jail are bad people. People who commit murder or steal or fight or have been drunk and disorderly. Little did we realize that later that day, it was Norma—their mother, not me—who would be arrested.

We had asked all of those who were willing to march to meet us at Shiloh Baptist Church early Monday morning. It had only been a few days since the Freedom Riders had been arrested. My wife, along with a few of her friends—Alma Chatmon, Anna Meeks, Marian King, Cora Powell, and others—were eager to help coordinate mass rallies and demonstrations. Norma and I took the lead as we marched with hundreds of others from Shiloh through Harlem en route to the city hall. There were many onlookers, including many policemen. Tensions began to mount as we continued up South Lee Street, approaching the business district. Curious Blacks and apprehensive Whites gazed in amazement as marchers continued into an uncertain fate. With each step, the tension continued to mount. Twice, we marched around without incident. We wrongly concluded that there would be no arrest on that day. I told Norma to lead them around one more time and then go straight to the church. I had to

The Battle Is Joined

return to my office, where a room full of patients was waiting to see me.

It was on the third march around the city square that an army of police, armed with billy clubs and loaded weapons, was waiting to arrest all in the march. Chief Pritchett stepped in front of the marchers with a bullhorn in hand and loudly announced, "You are all under arrest for unlawful marching without a permit."

Albany marchers dropped to their knees in front of City Hall to pray for freedom.

No one resisted arrest, and marchers were ushered into the jail cells. When the Albany city and county jails reached capacity, remaining marchers were loaded onto waiting buses and transported to other jails in the surrounding communities. Norma was among those arrested and jailed in nearby Lee County, one of the most notoriously racist counties in the state.

There had been numerous demonstrations in the form of picketing, with no more than four to eight people in a single block carrying signs encouraging people to boycott the stores in the city of Albany. This Monday morning march led by Norma marked the beginning of the series of marches that led to the arrest of more than a thousand willing volunteers.

William G Anderson, DO, FACOS

To be arrested was a different experience in Albany than in most other Southern communities in that the police chief had studied the life and works of Mahatma Gandhi. He well knew of the success of Gandhi in overthrowing the British regime in India without benefit of arms because of his nonviolent tactics. Chief Pritchett knew that to initiate violence on the part of his policemen could do nothing but aggravate the situation and call more press and worldwide attention to the Albany Movement. He directed his police staff and other police agencies from surrounding communities, who would also participate in arresting the demonstrators, that no violence would be tolerated.

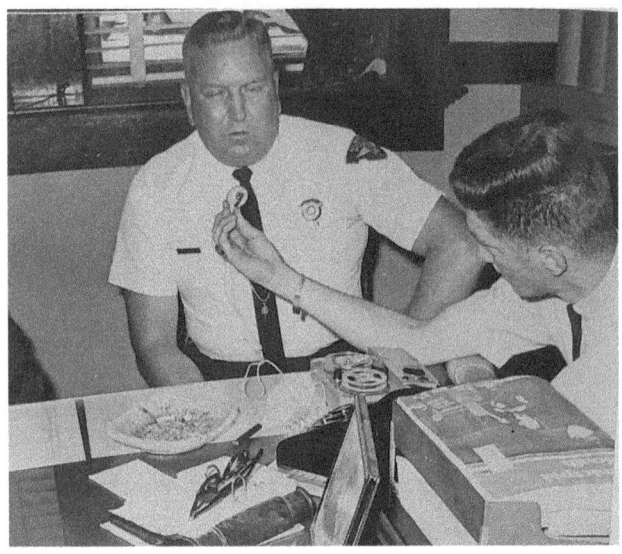

An inhibitor of violence in the Albany Movement was Police Chief Laurie Pritchett, who studied the principles of peaceful social change.

Events escalated quickly. On December 12th, students marched to protest the Freedom Riders' trial, and more than 260 were arrested. The next day, another 200 students were arrested for marching on City Hall without a permit.

The Albany Movement had been just organized, leadership had been selected, regular meetings were being held, and intermittent

The Battle Is Joined

mass rallies were beginning to progress to weekly activities. There was always a different preacher who would set the tone, followed by speeches from leaders of the movement, and usually culminating with my rousing, spirited address, urging people to boycott Albany businesses and to stay off the buses. The rallies would often go until the late hours of the night, but the people seemed not to tire. There had been many arrests, starting with those picketing more than four to eight in a city block, consistent with what would be acceptable not only under the constitution, but under general labor practices. Each day, there would be more demonstrations and more arrests to the point that there were several hundred people in jail with no preparation for their release. The movement had no money for bonds. The minimal legal representation, that was almost voluntary, was by Attorney C.B. King. The Albany Movement as an organization was certainly in its infancy and had not yet accumulated any funds.

Frustrations were high, the uncertainties of the movement were mounting, patience was wearing thin, and feelings of failure were setting in. My lack of experience in civil rights battles was beginning to show in my leadership, for I had few answers as to the next steps to take. With hundreds in jail, the constant threats on me and my family by the Ku Klux Klan, no money, limited support from the major civil rights organizations, scores of new people coming to Albany every day with no place to stay, and the rapidly growing focus of the world centered on Albany—it is no wonder that I was getting desperate.

It was at this point that I recalled the relationships that had been established between Martin Luther King Jr., Ralph David Abernathy, and me. The Montgomery bus boycott had been settled, and the Montgomery Improvement Association continued to be active. King and Abernathy moved to Atlanta, where they formed the Southern Christian Leadership Conference (SCLC).

So, this was my plan: to call in the big guns, an experienced organization with resources. Norma and I attended a meeting of the board of directors of the Albany Movement and indicated that we had a personal relationship with two of the best-known civil rights leaders in America at that time. There was some reluctance out of fear of a loss of identity from other civil rights organizations that were present. These organizations depended on their identity and the activity in which they were engaged to raise money to sustain the organizations, so it was understandable there was some hesitancy. There was the real fear that all the attention would be drawn to Dr. King and Rev. Abernathy and the SCLC and away from the other organizations present. Their fears were well-founded, but inescapable. I felt I had no alternative.

Norma and I called Martin and Ralph and asked that they come to Albany. Needless to say, Dr. King was reluctant to come under such circumstances, and he gave me every reason why he should not. He had commitments, literally, all over the world. He had addressed members of Congress. He had been the guest of the president and the attorney general of the United States. He had spoken at the most prestigious churches and synagogues in the United States and had been the guest of royalty. Why, then, should he come to a small town in southwest Georgia to join in what to many had been an ill-advised activity? If not ill-advised, it was then perhaps ill-timed, and if not ill-advised and ill-timed, then it was certainly an act without proper planning. We were guilty of all of those. My pleading was impassioned—no, desperate—for I was in a dilemma, up the proverbial creek without any visible means of propulsion. I was at a complete loss as to what to do.

It was coincidental that I placed the call at the time of a mass meeting, and the people were singing songs of freedom, and I said to Martin, "Just listen to them singing, Martin."

I held the phone out where he could hear the singing from the church filled with people. And as he heard those songs of freedom, I kept asking, "Do you hear them singing, Martin? They are begging. They are pleading. They need a leader. They want to be free and do not know how. They need you to come and lead them."

The Battle Is Joined

Honored to welcome Dr. King (left) and Rev. Abernathy (right) to my home.

Soon after, Martin and Ralph came with members of the SCLC staff. Martin came with the intention of giving a speech and returning to Atlanta.

The word quickly spread over southwest Georgia that The King was coming on December 15. People flocked to Albany from as far away as Columbus, Ohio; Savannah and Macon, Georgia; and Tallahassee, Florida. They came by the hundreds, overflowing Shiloh Baptist Church and Mt. Zion Baptist Church that were directly across the street from each other.

Martin first spoke at Shiloh to a capacity crowd. He was introduced by Ralph, who was one of the greatest warm-up preachers that the Baptist Church has ever produced. Ralph started with, "They call me an outside agitator. It bothered me at first because I thought an agitator was something negative or derogatory. But one day, I noticed my wife washing clothes. In the washing machine, there was this paddle going back and forth. I asked my wife, 'What is that?'

She responded, 'It's an agitator.'

'What does it do?'

She said, 'It gets the dirt out.'

Then I said, 'It's OK to call me an agitator. I'm proud to be an agitator because we have come here to get the dirt out of Albany.'"

The crowd roared; they loved him. Ralph was a warm, loving, and kind person, and the alter ego of Martin Luther King. Martin never made a major decision without first conferring with Ralph.

Martin spoke at Shiloh for about 20 minutes, a captivating and mesmerizing and motivating and stimulating speech, the likes of which we had never before heard. As he finished speaking and was returning to his seat, I said to him, "Martin, now you've got to go across the street to Mt. Zion Church."

He said, "But, Andy, I'm tired. I had a long day. I've been traveling for two weeks. I've given more than 25 speeches. I've met with dignitaries. I haven't seen my wife and kids in two weeks. I'm tired."

I said, "But Martin, the people across the street in Mt. Zion have been waiting a hundred years for a leader like you. They have come from hundreds of miles around, jeopardizing their personal safety and security just to hear you. You will have to speak to them."

Martin reluctantly crossed the street to Mt. Zion Baptist Church, where again Ralph warmed up the crowd and Martin spoke, again for 20 to 30 minutes. As he was returning to his seat at Mt. Zion, I leaned over and whispered in his ear, "Martin, you have to go back to Shiloh."

Whereupon he said, "Andy, I've already been there. I've already spoken there."

I said, "I know. But these are new people. These are people who could not get into the church, who could not get near the church when you spoke the first time. And they, too, have been waiting

The Battle Is Joined

hundreds of years for a leader like you to show them a way out of this racist environment."

Back he went across the street to Shiloh and spoke to a church filled to capacity, overflowing with people, with an energy that revitalized the nearly exhausted Dr. King. Of course, as he finished his third speech, I just smiled and looked at the door. He nodded. We walked across the street a second time to Zion.

Albany marchers were peaceful, restrained, and resolute.

Each time he preached, he got stronger and became committed to the people who were now carrying him. I knew right there and then that another stride toward freedom was being made. It was reported that I committed Martin to lead a march in Albany without having asked him in advance. I cannot deny the desire, but the intent I will deny, while taking great pride and satisfaction in the results. Dr. King led the first spontaneous mass march in Albany.

Martin Luther King Jr. came to Albany to make a single speech, but he was propelled into something much larger there. A few days later, he returned to Albany, where he led nearly 300 Black people in a march to pray in front of City Hall. All were arrested, including the leadership of the Albany Movement.

At the preceding rally, the people had been advised to come on

Saturday morning prepared to stay in jail for an indefinite period, for this was to be our greatest push in our fight to obtain freedom. The crowd was more excited than any time in the movement, as if they could sense a major victory. The atmosphere was electrifying, with speeches from Abernathy, King, me as president, Slater King as vice president, and local ministers, all of whom informed the attendees, who counted into the hundreds, to come on Saturday prepared to go into a future in which the only certainty was jail. There was not much sleeping done that night as the air was filled with excitement and anticipation of the events that were to come.

Early on Saturday morning, the crowd began to gather. There were old people and young people, men and women, boys and girls. They were dressed warmly. Some had snacks in their pockets. They had made preparations at home not to return at any specified time. They sang, "*Oh, oh, freedom! Oh, oh, freedom. Oh, oh, freedom over me. And before I'll be a slave, I'll be buried in my grave, and go home to my Lord and be free.*" And they sang, "*Ain't gonna let nobody turn me 'round. Ain't gonna let nobody turn me 'round.*" And they would call out to the sheriffs in unison, and they would say, "*Ain't gonna let Sheriff Chappell or Sheriff Campbell or Chief Pritchett turn me around.*"

These were people who were going on faith, with no promise of legal representation, unaware of the charges that would be brought against them, uncertain as to the outcome of court trials and, in some cases, even doubtful of their very survival. Many of those arrested were being sent to jails in all surrounding towns, and many of those had reputations for being very violent, even to the extent of lynching.

Never had I witnessed such courage, such will, and such determination from people who had everything to lose, including their lives, for never in history had this entrenched system of segregation and discrimination been so challenged. The laws of the state of Georgia that required segregation of the races, the long-standing practices of the state that prohibited Blacks from registering and voting, and the very foundations of racism in Albany and throughout the South were being shaken by this newly organized,

The Battle Is Joined

inexperienced, unsophisticated, independent, grassroots spontaneous movement. While many civil rights, social, and civic organizations became members of the Albany Movement, we had all agreed to subvert the independent identities for the sake of a goal unprecedented in the history of the Civil Rights Movement in America.

The march proceeded through Harlem from South Jackson Street, headed north, and crossed Oglethorpe, passing the yet-segregated bus station. There we found waiting for the marchers, lining both sides of the street, members of the National Guard. The Guard had been called out at the request of the city of Albany, and they came in battle fatigues, heavily armed with rifles, side arms, and bayonets. We never knew for sure whether or not they had live ammunition in the chamber of the guns, but it was quite apparent that live ammunition was readily available on their artillery belts. Added to the local policemen, there were hundreds of uniformed National Guard soldiers who lined the streets of Albany from Harlem to the City Hall.

With bullhorn in hand, Chief Laurie Pritchett ordered all marchers to stop and to return to the church, or they would be arrested. The march was being led by me, locked arm in arm with Martin Luther King Jr. Immediately behind us was my wife Norma, locking arms with Ralph David Abernathy. Hundreds of people followed including Slater and Marian King, members of SNCC, CORE, Urban League, NAACP, and others, and the numbers were growing the further we marched downtown. One of the soldiers raised his rifle in the ready-arms position and stepped in front of Dr. King and me. He announced, "Stop this march now." He raised the rifle as though he were about to strike one of us. I said to the National Guardsman, who appeared to be quite young and inexperienced, "If you hit anyone in this line, hit me first." I stared him directly in the eye.

My wife, very quietly behind me, said, "Shut up."

Dr. King and Dr. Abernathy remained silent, ready to proceed with the march. The young National Guardsman promptly put the rifle down, stepped aside, and we proceeded to march to City Hall.

As we arrived, throngs of policemen from in and around Albany were prepared to arrest each and every one of us, and to shuffle us off to every available jail space within a radius of 50 miles. King, Abernathy, and I were selected to go to Americus.

I thought, *How fortuitous. Americus, the place I was born and reared, my hometown.*

We were transported under rather heavy guard, including members of the FBI, whom we distrusted very much, as we had every reason to believe that Director J. Edgar Hoover intended to kill the Civil Rights Movement, painting us as members of the Communist Party and as subversives who would, in fact, destroy the American society.

Some of the FBI agents we had gotten to know on a rather personal basis because not only were they assigned to my home, but also whenever Martin Luther King Jr. and Ralph David Abernathy came to town, they would be assigned to them. These FBI agents had a difficult time relating to a man of the stature of Martin Luther King Jr. On one occasion while in jail in Albany, one of the FBI agents whom, ironically, I can recall by only his last name of Hubble, constantly referred to Dr. King as "King." At one point after Hubble repeatedly had done this, Dr. King paused and said, "Brother Hubble, you don't know me well enough to call me 'King.'"

Agent Hubble looked as though he was trying to find the nearest hole in the ground to crawl into. He had never been more embarrassed and humiliated by a Black man who was obviously his intellectual, emotional, and spiritual superior. Never again, at least in our presence, did Agent Hubble refer to Dr. King as "King."

The three of us arrived in Americus at the Sumter County Jail, where we were greeted by the notorious Sheriff Fred Chappell, whose first remarks were, "All right, boys, take off your hats. You're in my jail now."

It was not too bad as jails go, for it was relatively new, the

The Battle Is Joined

mattresses were yet clean, and the food was not bad. Needless to say, I had never anticipated being in jail in my hometown for anything. By this time, I was completely exhausted, having gone for days and nights without a peaceful night's sleep.

Once in the Americus/Sumter County jail, my exhaustion came down on me like a ton of bricks, and for the first hours, I had a fitful sleep, and I could imagine the people singing the songs of freedom. I would occasionally call Martin or Ralph and ask, "Don't you hear those children singing? Can't you hear those children singing?" That was music to my imaginary ear.

A focal point of the Albany Movement was at our home. Norma and I welcomed many guests and hosted the occasional media conference at our picnic table: (left to right) me, Dr. King, and Dr. Abernathy.

I was never more at peace than I was at the moment, knowing that I had done all I could do for the advancement of my people, to liberate them from the bondages of a virtual and a literal slavery. Members of the press present, when they witnessed my appearance of peace and, on occasion, even exhilaration, enjoying the satisfaction of what I considered a very successful nonviolent demonstration, reported that this was not realistic for one to have such joy in the midst of such conflict. To this day, it's been difficult for me to describe the breadth and depth of that peace.

We stayed in jail all Saturday night and all day Sunday, and on early Monday morning, we were escorted back to Albany for trial in the court of Judge Abner Israel. The Albany city attorney, with his limited knowledge of the law but with his stern commitment and conviction that the system of segregation and discrimination must be preserved, placed the charges before the court. It was at this point that the now-selected biracial committee—Solomon Walker, Benny Frank Cochran, and Thomas Chatmon—were in session with the chief of police. It was from those sessions that verbal agreements were made and the joint press conference was given, immediately followed by reneging on the part of the city. The result was that, after months of demonstrations culminating with the mass march, we came out of jail with a verbal commitment that would not be honored.

Blacks boycott Albany businesses during the Christmas season.

Albany was only different in that many local merchants had either gone bankrupt or were on the verge of bankruptcy. It was near the Christmas season when historically and traditionally, all of the merchants gladly received their Black customers and patrons. This

The Battle Is Joined

was entirely lacking in the season of Christmas 1961. Most of the Blacks went to other towns, especially Moultrie, which was a short 25 miles away, to do all of their Christmas shopping. Also, many Whites stayed from town out of fear of the demonstrations occurring that may lead to violence.

At the end of a trial that may be characterized as a kangaroo court, those arrested were slowly released on "straw" bonds. These bonds required no cash, just a signature indicating that they would return for trial, but there was also the verbal commitment that none of those arrested would ever be brought to trial. The only persons tried on that date were King, Abernathy, and me, and a verdict was never rendered. Immediately following the court appearance, we met with our lawyers, where Dr. King indicated his discomfort with the conditions of the release, and expressed a desire to remain in jail until such time as there was an appropriate resolution by the City Council—a resolution that was never forthcoming. Dr. King and members of the SCLC staff returned to Atlanta for a much-needed rest. Norma and I, with our children, went to Atlanta for a short visit with her mother and her two brothers, James and Charle, and her sister Juanita.

The Albany Movement and the NAACP

The national NAACP was somewhat reluctant to come to Albany because the movement started with no plans whatsoever. The local chapter, however, was represented and, to its credit, had not assumed or insisted on a leadership role. They were eager to be a part of the movement. Thomas Chatmon and Ed Hamilton, among other local leaders, were greatly responsible for the NAACP's involvement in the movement's activities.

It was still early in the fall of 1961 when SNCC had come to Albany and had recruited many students from the local high schools, and some from Albany State College, and a series of events was taking place all over the city. There was picketing in downtown, protesting discrimination and segregation in the stores and businesses, and also protests against the denial of the city to grant Blacks the right to register and vote. The arrests up until this time were sporadic and usually involved only a few people. It was not until the Freedom Riders came to town that large numbers of Blacks got involved and attended the mass rallies, and the marches became larger, and more people were arrested. Several hundred people were in jail by the time the NAACP national headquarters in New York had heard of this local, spontaneous, uncoordinated movement.

This is not to say that the NAACP was not represented in Albany in that Thomas Chatmon, a highly respected local businessman, had organized and supervised a youth chapter of the NAACP. There was an adult chapter headed by a Black minister. These local chapters had not become actively involved in the picketing and mass demonstrations, as this was not the accepted policy of the national organization.

When Martin Luther King Jr. and Ralph David Abernathy came to Albany and with the force and impact of the Southern Christian Leadership Conference, national—and soon international—attention was brought to Albany. This became the focal point of the Civil Rights Movement in the nation. This was the first grassroots, spontaneous, unorganized mass picket protest demonstration in the history of the Civil Rights Movement of this era.

With the world's attention on Albany, the NAACP hierarchy sensed the necessity of becoming involved. Orders were sent from New York to the Atlanta regional office. Ruby Hurley was the regional secretary for the entire southeastern United States. Vernon Jordan, a young lawyer who practiced with the leading civil rights lawyer of the South, Don Hollowell, in Atlanta, was her assistant. At the direction of the national office, Hurley and Jordan came to Albany.

The Battle Is Joined

Leading the next generation into freedom: Thomas Chatmon (right) organized a youth chapter of the NAACP in Albany.

They attended a mass meeting and thereafter joined us at one of our regularly scheduled strategy sessions. I was greeted by Ruby Hurley with: "You see what kind of mess you've got these people in now?"

I said, "Yes, Miss Hurley. I know what kind of trouble I've gotten these people in. What I would like to know is how to get them out of trouble."

She proceeded to explain the policies and practices of the NAACP. Their focus was on the ballot and boycott. She indicated the NAACP had been very successful with these strategies.

Notwithstanding the criticism of the NAACP and the reluctance of the national organization to join in with the Albany Movement, we continued our nightly mass rallies and daily demonstrations in the form of picketing or marching. The NAACP elected to become a part of the organization and encouraged their Hollowell to help our local Black lawyer, C.B. King. For the first time we had cooperation, if not the total commitment, of the NAACP in the Albany Movement.

Roy Wilkins, the executive director of the NAACP, requested a meeting with me in New York. So, off I went, and from that point, the NAACP was an official part of the Albany Movement. Now there was

William G Anderson, DO, FACOS

SNCC, Congress on Racial Equality (CORE), Urban League, the Southern Christian Leadership Conference, and several local social and civic organizations. The Albany Movement was a well-established organization with a name, headquarters, legal representation, and organized volunteer carpool, elected officers, and the most highly visible civil rights leaders of the era, Martin Luther King Jr. and Ralph David Abernathy.

Ruby Hurley was a stately, well-dressed woman who exuded confidence and was able to quickly analyze a critical situation and determine what course of action was to be taken. In her presence, one got the feeling that she was looking down her nose at those of us who were neophytes in the civil rights struggle, and we had to confess that she was right. We did not have the knowledge, the experience, the resources, or the backing of a major civil rights organization at that time. All we had was a desire to be free, to be liberated from the tyranny of oppression and the denial of basic human rights, to include the right to register and vote. We could not argue with her assessment of the situation in which we found ourselves, but we found plenty to argue about how to get out of this dilemma. We all got the impression that Hurley wasn't in Albany by her choosing or election, but that she was there because she had been directed by the national office that said, "There can be no major civil rights activity again in the United States without NAACP involvement." The national headquarters remembered its reluctance to get involved in the Montgomery bus boycott that was eminently successful and led by a group of civil rights neophytes, namely, King and Abernathy. I do not believe the NAACP wanted to make the same mistake twice.

Vernon Jordan was a tall, strapping, impressive-looking young man. While fresh out of law school, with limited experience with the NAACP, he was firmly grounded in the law office of Don Hollowell. Vernon was quiet during the initial meeting with the NAACP hierarchy, but he was quite observant, and I could tell he had ideas of his own. He soon became an integral part of the Albany Movement and was actively involved in all legal matters that related

The Battle Is Joined

to our activity. Vernon later became the director of the Urban League and subsequently had his talents recognized when he was named to President William Jefferson Clinton's transition committee.

Ruby Hurley was noticeably absent for the remainder of the period of high activity with mass demonstrations and arrests. We were of the opinion that she had been recalled from Albany because of her somewhat aloof appearance, negative critical analysis of what had transpired, and her desire to "take over" rather than become a part of the Albany Movement.

I would be remiss not to mention the presence of the nationally known civil rights Attorney, William Kunstler. Kunstler voluntarily came to Albany and was a welcomed part of the legal team representing the movement. He stayed for several weeks at a time and worked closely with attorneys King, Hollowell, Jordan, and a number of other itinerant lawyers from New York, Chicago, and Detroit. These lawyers traveled at their own expense and, for the most part, made no demands for compensation for their services.

The Albany Movement and the Courts

Hundreds of people of all ages, from all aspects of life—business and professional people, students, and everyday hard-working men and women—were arrested. At the height of the movement, there were more than a thousand incarcerated at one time. Because this far exceeded the capacity of the jails in Albany, the county jail had accepted the overflow, followed by expansion to every jail in southwest Georgia, including Columbus, Camilla, Waycross, Americus, Dawson, and Newton. Every jail within 50 miles was filled to capacity.

During this time, the city of Albany was virtually paralyzed; there was no activity in town. Blacks would not come to town to purchase, and Whites would not come to town out of fear of being caught up in a mass demonstration that might lead to violence. Although the police chief forbade violence against the demonstrators, it was obvious that the demonstrators had a tremendous impact on both the economy and the social life of the people of Albany.

A significant product of the Albany Movement was a positive change in self-perception among the community's Black people.

At the height of the demonstrations, with more than 1,000 Blacks in jail, the City Council appeared to capitulate to allow a biracial commission to be formed. However, the council wanted to select not only the members that would represent the White establishment, but they also wanted to select the Blacks. This, of course, was rejected. However, the Albany Movement did agree to send a delegation composed of Benny Frank Cochran, Thomas Chatmon, and Solomon Walker. The City Council would not meet with the representatives from the Black committee but rather delegated that responsibility to the chief of police, who was designated as a spokesman for the City Council.

Pressure was mounting on the city with more demonstrations planned, with thousands of students from the Northeast coming to town to participate in the demonstrations, with Christmas approaching and with these students agreeing to spend Christmas in jail for the cause of freedom. With these threats hanging over the

The Battle Is Joined

heads of the City Council and the city of Albany, a verbal agreement was reached with the Albany Movement. The operative word here is "verbal," for at no time would the City Council put any agreements in writing and had already demonstrated that they could not be trusted.

The alternative was suggested of a joint press release spelling out the terms by which those arrested would be released. The terms were very simple. One: all of the prisoners would be released unconditionally (the city had insisted on including straw bonds, meaning that bonds would never be called). Two: none of the demonstrators would be prosecuted. Three: the buses would be desegregated. Four: a permanent biracial committee would be appointed. Martin Luther King Jr. and I were the last to agree to this settlement without a formal declaration by members of the City Council, yet we were convinced that there was at least an element of integrity in that they would not renege after making the public statement to the press. Sadly, our naivete and inexperience in dealing in such civil rights matters were never more evident than when we, although reluctantly, accepted the verbal agreement to come out of jail on a promise.

Our recent experiences with the city should have been a clear indication that they were not to be trusted. On numerous occasions, those arrested were taken to court for trial before Judge Abner Israel, who would limit the debate of the lawyers representing the Albany Movement, including C.B. King, Don Hollowell, and even Constance Baker Motley. Judge Israel would permit them to make their presentations, but he would apparently take a nap on the bench.

At the conclusion of the pleadings, the judge would be awakened, and he would ask, "Are you through, C.B.?" whereupon Attorney King would respond, "I am finished, Your Honor."

Then Judge Israel would say, without having left the bench, "Here's my decision." The decision of guilty was already written and prepared for publication prior to the trial. This was not unusual, but rather the pattern for those of us who found ourselves in the city courts of Albany.

The federal court in the district of J. Robert Elliott, Federal

District Court judge, was a bit more sophisticated, yet the results were as predictable as in the courts of Albany.

The city attorney had filed a petition and was granted an injunction that prohibited us from further demonstrations on the grounds that they posed a threat to the community and violated local ordinances. Notwithstanding the fact that we were exercising constitutionally

guaranteed rights, the restraining order was issued. We attempted to appeal the order to the Federal District Court, that of J. Robert Elliott. Judge Elliott suddenly became unavailable, and could not be reached at his office, at his home, or by any other means. It was apparent that Judge Elliott did not want to deal with this matter. We therefore were forced to carry our petition to lift the injunction to Elbert Tuttle, the chief judge of the Federal District Court in Atlanta. While a Southerner, Judge Tuttle was also a very brilliant lawyer who had the utmost respect for law. He was committed to upholding the U.S. Constitution and guaranteeing the protection of its inherent rights.

The group of representatives from the Albany Movement included Attorneys C.B. King and Don Hollowell and was led by Attorney Constance Baker Motley, who was very much experienced not only in constitutional law, but also in appearing before federal courts. The attorney general of Georgia pulled out all of the stops and called on the best legal minds in the state, even going to the law schools of Emory University and the University of Georgia. The state sought to prove that the activities in which the Albany Movement was engaged were detrimental to the peace, safety, and tranquility of the people of Albany, and in fact was wielding irreparable harm to the economy. This argument was supported by several cases that were cited by the attorney representing the state and the city, and duly noted by Judge Tuttle.

Following the presentation by the attorneys for the state of Georgia, Attorney Constance Baker Motley took the floor. I had never witnessed a more brilliant, forceful, impressive, and persuasive argu-

The Battle Is Joined

ment in support of our petition to lift the injunction than that presented by Attorney Motley. She frequently referenced each case that had been cited by the attorneys representing the state. In each case, without exception, she went on to prove that the decisions in the lower courts either had been overturned on appeal or later dismissed. Not a single case stated by the attorneys for the state of Georgia was able to withstand this kind of scrutiny, and I have never been more proud to be represented in a court of law. This was a major victory for the Albany Movement, and we were free to return to Albany to continue our peaceful protest demonstrations.

At the time, we did not anticipate another tactic that would be taken by the law enforcement officials of Albany: to attack individually the leadership of the Albany Movement.

On January 3rd, the Albany City Council voted five to two to deny the Albany Movement's request for a biracial commission and negotiations. This southwest Georgia town, deeply rooted in the tradition of segregation and discrimination, was not willing to enter into negotiations with local Black leaders to find common ground whereby we could bring an end to this system that had held both Blacks and Whites as captives. We were all captives in that people of neither race could freely move or live or work with the other because of legal, social or traditional barriers. As an active member of the Criterion Club and the Washington Heights Improvement Association, I, along with four others, was selected to petition the City Council to establish a biracial commission to study the means by which we could bring an end to this system. The City Council, as all other elected and appointed officers, was lily-White. At no time did a Black have the opportunity to serve in any capacity within the city. A petition was presented through the mayor's office prior to the City Council formal meeting.

I had just returned from vacation with my wife and children at Atlantic Beach. This beach was owned by the Afro-American Insurance Company and was the only beach that welcomed Black tourists. While driving back to Albany with my family, a state patrolman stopped us, and I was charged with crossing the yellow line on the highway, an infraction that was, for all intents and purposes, void. We were the only automobile for miles around. I challenged the state patrolman on his decision to give me a ticket, and I indicated that I would report him to the AAA, my insurer, whereupon he remarked, "You can report me to the AAA or the NAACP, but you're going to jail."

I was escorted to the local county jail, where I was summarily locked up without a hearing and without the opportunity to post bond. My wife and children were left in the automobile crying, concerned for my safety. As it was not too unusual for Blacks to be arrested in the South, and escorted away to prison, never to be heard from again, we had every reason to believe many such Blacks were executed by lynching. The sheriff of the county was somewhat more educated than the state patrolman and more sensitive to my family's concerns. As good fortune would have it, he came to the jail and saw my wife and children in the car crying and asked what the problem was. They told him that I had been arrested for having crossed a yellow line on the highway. He came into the jail, had me released, and permitted me to post a bond. However, he assured me that the fine would be the same as the amount of the bond, which was $50, and therefore, it was pointless for me to post the bond and return for a court hearing. Having no choice and desiring to get out of jail and return to my family, I posted the $50 bond, knowing that it would be the last time I would see that money and that I had no intentions of returning to this rural county for trial.

We returned to Albany late Sunday evening, and I went to my office on Monday morning and, as was usually the case, I had a large number of patients. At the end of the day, I decided to go to the City Council meeting to get a response to our petition. I sat in the back of the chambers, in a section reserved just for Blacks. I was the only Black in the room, and I sat throughout the formal proceedings. At the end the mayor announced that the council meeting was adjourned. I stood up and asked to be heard. I was granted permis-

The Battle Is Joined

sion, and politely inquired as to the disposition of the petition that had been presented by the committee representing the Black community. The mayor stated that the petition had been presented to the City Council in closed session, and a determination had been made that there were no common grounds for agreement. Therefore, we would not receive a response.

I promptly left the council chambers. My leaving must have been somewhat noticeable because the following day in the local newspaper, *The Albany Herald*, there was a front-page story relating the brief encounter with the City Council. In bold print, the headlines read "Negro Doctor Demands Immediate Integration of Albany." The article went on to describe who I was, where I lived, my phone number, my address, and where my office could be located. Needless to say, this was designed to threaten and intimidate the patients whom I served and me. The word spread throughout the community, and many Blacks who were employed by Whites were threatened with the loss of their jobs. Many who had mortgages were threatened with foreclosures. Loans and credit were denied and, in essence, economic sanctions were placed on Blacks in an attempt to derail this Civil Rights Movement.

My family was threatened constantly. We received numerous phone calls indicating that the Ku Klux Klan was coming to kill us, that we would be run out of town, and that I would not be permitted to practice as I would have no patients. The response of the Blacks in Albany was heartening. At no point did my practice suffer; if anything, my practice increased. My patients demonstrated the kind of commitment and devotion that every physician desires to have. Many of my patients offered to protect me and, in fact, on frequent occasions, would escort me on house calls and would surround my home to make certain that my family and I were safe. What was not generally known was that many of those who offered to protect me were both well-armed and possibly not as committed to nonviolence as Martin Luther King Jr.

On one memorable night, the Ku Klux Klan was having a massive rally one-half block from my home. When I arrived from my office it was night, and my home was completely surrounded by Blacks who, I knew, were heavily armed. They told me, "Go in and enjoy your dinner, Doctor, and go to bed and have a good night's sleep. You will not be bothered in any way by the Klan."

As I ate my dinner, I could hear the Klan shouting epithets and admonishing one another of the dangers of this Civil Rights Movement. They would scream questions like, "Do you want your daughter to marry one of Anderson's children? We must stop these niggas before they take over this town."

I could see the flames from the burning cross, close enough to my home to feel the heat. I could see shadows of the hooded Klansmen as they milled around in the hundreds. Ironically, I had lost all fear. It was my wife's grandmother, whom we affectionately called Sugar, who had asked, "William, don't you know that they will kill you for what you're doing?"

I said, "Yes, Sugar, I know that I might be killed, but if it happens, I will feel as though my life was not in vain." Yes, I was prepared to die for this cause. It's not that I do not love life. I loved life then, as I always have and always will, but I felt that this was the time when I had to take a stand. It was fortunate that my wife was willing to make a similar sacrifice, for it was she who was the first to go to jail. In addition, it was most difficult to keep my teenage children, especially Laurita, my number one daughter, from going to jail. It was often much more than I thought I could possibly bear when my wife and I were both in jail and fearing for the safety of my children.

The Dawn Of 1962: Success And Exhaustion

On January 9, 1962, the work of the young people of SNCC was validated. U.S. District Judge W.A. Bootle declared racial segregation in voting procedures in Albany and Dougherty County unconstitutional. Three days later, on January 12, Ola Mae Quarterman was arrested for refusing to give up her seat on a city bus to a White

The Battle Is Joined

person. In response, the Albany Movement launched a boycott of the bus system and other businesses.

I had to admit that we in the Albany Movement had made many, many mistakes because of our inexperience, and that we were overzealous in that we did not select a single target but rather attacked every vestige of segregation and discrimination in the city. We decided to boycott the buses, in addition to all stores in downtown Albany. We, the leadership of the Albany Movement, had decided that we would use this success as a weapon in the fight against other aspects of segregation and discrimination, as the city had depended heavily on bus transportation.

We selected the city bus service, remembering that the buses had been the focal point of the successful Montgomery, Alabama, boycott just a few years earlier. We did not think that it would be easy, but we believed that if Montgomery could do it, then Albany could do it. Yet there were many Blacks that depended solely upon the bus system to get to and from the places of employment. Not unlike in the Montgomery bus boycott, carpools were formed all over town and many people walked to their jobs. Many Blacks had automobiles in Albany, and Blacks owned gas stations, and they were willing—no, eager—to get involved.

Ironically, a number of Whites, fearing being without their Black maids, cooks, and butlers, would arrange to pick them up personally. They were only willing to sacrifice so much to protect this system of segregation and discrimination. They were certainly not willing to give up their maid service.

The young Rev. Joe Smith was more than a passive supporter. He coordinated efforts and was among the first to volunteer to drive in the carpool.

On February 1st, we had ample evidence of the success of our boycott. The Albany bus station closed. The local bus company, soon after the boycott became effective, hired a Black bus driver and there was no longer discrimination on the buses.

It was in the winter of 1962 that I reached a point of exhaustion that led to my leaving Albany for a few days for rest and for recuperation. I checked into the Veterans Hospital facility in Tuskegee, Alabama, where I felt most comfortable, for by this time, my name was well known as a troublemaker and I was probably not welcomed at White-owned and operated facilities. After a few days at Veterans, I went to visit with Norma's grandparents in Sylacauga, Alabama. Norma's grandparents were the grand patriarch and matriarch of the Dixon/Shepard family.

Granddaddy Shepard was a highly respected pastor and preacher in Alabama, who had been at the same church for over forty years and had held many offices within the Alabama State Baptist Convention. He also was a member of the board of trustees and a strong supporter of Selma University in Selma, Alabama. Selma would later become one of the major battlefields for the civil rights movement.

Grandma Shepard was given the nickname "Sugar" by our children, and the name stuck, perhaps because it was easy to remember and it suited her personality. She was a superb homemaker and cook, capable of preparing a meal fit for a king with little notice. I always looked forward to the opportunity to visit Granddad and Grandmamma Shepard as I could call her only a couple of hours in advance to tell her what I would want for dinner. That would usually include homemade rolls and peach cobbler pie. It never ceased to amaze me and others how quickly she could prepare such a meal without the benefit of modern conveniences. She cooked on an iron wood stove and without any electrical appliances. Light was provided by oil lamps and heat by an open fireplace or a potbelly stove. There was also no running water in the house, but these did not seem to affect the Shepards. They were as loving and supporting grandparents as any. I found a considerable amount of comfort being in their presence.

After a few days of rest and recuperation in Tuskegee and Sylacauga, I returned to Albany to resume my activities as the president of the Albany Movement. By this time, I had experienced a weight loss of about 30 pounds, because eating was the furthest thing from

The Battle Is Joined

my mind, and what little I did eat was immediately consumed by the extraordinary activity of my practice and long hours of strategy session meetings, nightly mass meetings and daily demonstrations.

On February 27, 1962, Dr. King returned to Albany for trial and was found guilty of disorderly conduct and parading without a permit. Sentencing was delayed until July 10, when he and the Rev. Abernathy were sentenced to pay a fine of $178 or complete 45 days of hard labor. They chose jail time. The next day, demonstrations protesting the arrests continued, and rock-throwing by some onlookers prompted Albany Police Chief Pritchett to ask the Movement for our cooperation in enforcing nonviolence rules. On July 13, King and Abernathy were released after a "well-dressed black man" paid the fine. It was later revealed that the bailout was actually paid by B.C. Gardner, a local White attorney.

Chief Laurie Pritchett (left) escorted Drs. King, Anderson, and Rev. Abernathy to jail.

William G Anderson, DO, FACOS

Federal Judge Robert Elliot issued an injunction against further demonstrations in Albany, with King and others specifically forbidden to march. In response, on July 22, Rev. Samuel Wells led a demonstration without King, and nearly 200 people were arrested. Violence ensued and Dr. King called for a "Day of Penance." Finally, on July 25, Federal Judge Elbert Tuttle overthrew Elliot's injunction, and a group of 217 people were arrested for conducting a prayer meeting in front of City Hall. On July 29, I found myself doing something I never expected, in a place I never expected, being interviewed on *Meet the Press*.

Notwithstanding the internal conflict that existed within Chief Pritchett, he proceeded to arrest me along with King and Abernathy. It was on a Saturday evening following a demonstration that the three of us were escorted from our jail cell to the chief's office. We soon discovered there had been numerous phone calls from *Meet the Press*. The calls included one from Lawrence Spivak, who was a producer. Dr. King was scheduled to be on *Meet the Press*, not anticipating that he would be in jail on the date he was to appear. Chief Pritchett was eager for us to come out of jail because the attention of the nation and much of the world was drawn to Albany, especially when Dr. King was in jail.

We indicated that Dr. King had made a commitment to the people of Albany that he would not come out of jail until our demand was met; the simple demand of appointment of a biracial committee to study the problems of segregation in Albany.

We returned to our cells and gave further consideration to the invitation from Lawrence Spivak. After much discussion, we concluded that it was far too important for our cause to tell the nation of the plight of Negroes in Albany and elsewhere in the South. We should not pass up the opportunity to be on *Meet the Press*. King, Abernathy, and I concluded that one of us should leave jail and go to New York to do the interview. We drew straws and mine was the short one.

When I came out of jail, I was briefed by Dr. King's staff, which

The Battle Is Joined

included Wyatt T. Walker, Andrew Young, Bernard Lee and others. In New York I was met by King's staff and escorted to a hotel where I was further briefed on what to expect from the interview. Some staff members of *Meet the Press* were not as sympathetic to the cause of civil rights as others. One staffer was well known for being against the Civil Rights Movement and he frequently wrote against it in his publications.

Nonetheless, I felt blessed that I could carry the message, that the interview went well, and the nation had an opportunity to hear what was happening in Albany. I returned to Albany with renewed vigor, encouraged by the positive response to the *Meet the Press* interview. I immediately became engaged in more demonstrations, to the point of exhaustion.

On January 31, 1962, the Albany City Council voted five to two to deny the Albany Movement's request for a biracial committee and negotiations.

On July 31, Chief Pritchett sought another federal court injunction, telling the court that his department had arrested eleven hundred demonstrators since December. On August 4, 1962, city officials claimed that by "firm and fair law enforcement," they had "broken the back" of the Albany Movement, and that the movement was "caused by no more than 30 professional civil rights workers." King commented that "segregation is on its deathbed in Albany, and the only thing uncertain about it is how costly the City Commission will make the funeral."

It was early in 1962 that the mass demonstrations ceased. There were only sporadic episodes of demonstrations and arrests. The Black community was somewhat disappointed in the outcome of the demonstrations and court trials in that our objectives of desegregating Albany apparently had failed. To the casual observer, the Albany Movement was a failure, and, as a matter of fact, much of the press characterized it as one of Martin Luther King Jr.'s failures. But for those of us who lived in Albany knew that it could not have been a failure because of the physical changes that we saw in our city that were paled by the changes in perceptions and attitudes of both the Whites and Blacks in Albany, a city which had elected to close its public libraries and parks and zoo rather than desegregate.

Most of the city businesses were suffering economically, for even though the demonstrations were much less frequent, the people were very slow in returning to shopping in Albany. Many businesses that could not withstand this amount of lost revenue were forced out. The city buses, which were desegregated, appeared to be returning to somewhat normal operations.

Those who look upon the Albany Movement as a failure need look no further than the changes in the perceptions and attitudes of the Blacks and Whites of Albany. The Blacks had discovered that they had the power to effect change and could do it nonviolently. They also had made a determination that at no time in the future would they ever accept the system of segregation and discrimination and that they would continue to press for the right to register and vote.

Whites, as a result of the Albany Movement, came to the realization that Blacks were not happy and content with things as they were and were not going to accept it anymore. As reluctant as they were to make a change, they knew after the movement that change was essential to the survival of Albany as a growing, prospering city.

The Albany Movement was extremely important in subsequent civil rights movements throughout the United States, especially in Birmingham and the Selma to Montgomery march. Birmingham was a turning point in the Civil Rights Movement in that all of the evil, vicious, relentless violent forces of the racists were unleashed. Bull Connor, the police chief, did not heed the warnings of Chief Laurie Pritchett to restrain his police from perpetrating any violent acts on the demonstrators. Chief Connor in Birmingham and Sheriff Jim Clark in Selma, Alabama, took a totally different tack with the determination that they could stop the demonstrations and kill the spirit of the movement by acts of violence. Beatings with billy clubs, showering with forcible water cannons, attacks by vicious dogs, and tram-

The Battle Is Joined

pling under the hooves of horses were tactics used by Chief Connor and Sheriff Clark. These acts of violence did nothing more than intensify the resolve of the demonstrators and call the attention of the world to the plights of Negroes throughout the South and in many parts of this nation.

Albany was the proving ground for the subsequent demonstrations in Montgomery and Selma. We learned how to return hate with love. We learned how to accept brutality and not fight back. We learned how to be passive and yet be strong. We learned that good would eventually triumph over evil.

The transition of Albany from the early racist city that it was to a more open and free society, extending certain basic and fundamental rights to Blacks, was a slow but certain process. Whether to avoid further confrontation with mass demonstrations, whether it was because the eyes of the world were on Albany, or whether it was out of a change of heart, Albany changed. One must return to Albany a few short years later to find Blacks in every city and county position, serving on the City Council, police force, sheriff's staff, and as judges and jurors. Blacks are present in all business and industry in Albany, and there is no obvious segregation and discrimination. Albany is a testament to the power of nonviolent movement.

Music Of The Civil Rights Movement

No history of the Civil Rights Movement could be complete without reference to the music of the era. Songs that were sung more often than not were a cappella, for we did not depend on the instrument to convey the message or tell the story of the events that were unfolding. The songs served more than a single purpose. Certainly they were entertaining and inspirational, but also they provided an opportunity for everyone to actively participate, for there was not a single person at a civil rights mass rally who did not join in the freedom songs.

The participation in the singing was not dependent on the quality of your singing voice, for that was totally irrelevant. No one was ever excluded from singing a freedom song because they could not sing on key or could not carry a tune. After all, these were not just songs, but they were messages, they were expressions of feelings, of frustration, of a yearning to be heard, of a burning desire to be free, of a willingness to make a sacrifice, even a supreme sacrifice, for the strong principles for which we were fighting. The freedom songs were a vital part of every mass meeting and our marching on that route to freedom.

Music was vital to both unity and expression in the Albany Movement. James Chadwell led the church choir.

They became "freedom songs" in the early 1950s, but you would hear very similar, if not identical, songs from the slave ships and the cotton fields and the auction blocks and the dungeons—all the places where Black people were held in bondage, bartered, sold and traded as cattle, bowed under the whips of slave masters, brutalized by slave mistresses, and raped by men with no desire to be fathers but just to find sexual gratification without responsibility. There were songs emanating from all of these events and situations that were not then called "freedom songs," they were the songs of slavery. Songs were even more essential in slavery, as there was no convenient means of communication. Slaves could not read or write, but their means of expression as their feelings of helplessness and hopelessness could only be expressed in song. The messages were quite strong to those who would hear. Hundreds of years later, those slave songs became freedom songs that carried similar messages that all said that we want to be free.

The original institutionally recognized Freedom Singers originated in Albany, in December 1962, led by Bernice Johnson, Rutha Harris, and others active in the Albany Movement. This was not a well-organized, well-trained, professional group. These were Black young men and women of Albany who had a message to tell, a message for the soul of the movement. The words would always convey a very visible picture of conditions that existed at the height of the movement. The songs were without title yet with a clear message that spoke of our yearning to be free. They captured many of the figures who were involved in the movement, including Chief Laurie Pritchett, Mayor Asa Kelley, Bunny Pritchett, and many others who represented the oppressors. These songs are best captured in books written by Bernice Johnson Reagon and Wyatt T. Walker and continue to be sung by the Freedom Singers, who have endured now for nearly a half-century.

Closing Out Our Time In Albany

A very interesting phenomenon occurred in 1963. The wives of three leaders in the Civil Rights Movement, Dr. King, Andy Young, and myself, all gave birth to daughters during the year. It wasn't until many years later that the three daughters met each other and discovered their commonality.

Phoebe Putney Hospital was the only hospital in Albany, and the only accommodations for Negroes were in the basement, where patients had to compete with the laundry, steam, water, and sewage pipes. These were not ideal conditions for any patients. We elected to have our child at home. Norma went to my friend Willie Reese for her prenatal care and delivery. The delivery was uneventful and our fifth and last child, Damita Dawn, became known as one of the "movement babies." She was a delight from birth and has been as close to a perfect child as any parent would ever want.

I was soon confronted with another lawsuit. This time I was charged with obstruction of justice, and in essence, of attempting to overthrow the government by leading protest demonstrations. Also, a local White merchant, who operated a grocery store in Harlem, charged me and leadership of the Albany Movement with threatening and endangering his customers and his business. This suit would later be tried in Albany and subsequently in Detroit after I moved to continue my studies in a surgical residency.

The Move Back North
1963–1967

During 1963, the Albany Movement had, for all practical purposes, ended its series of demonstrations. I felt that it was time for me to return to my studies and pursue my dream of becoming a surgeon. I first applied to Flint Osteopathic Hospital in Michigan, where I had served my internship and felt that I had the best opportunity of being selected. My record there had been impeccable and unblemished. In all modesty, I do not believe there had been a better-trained or a more dedicated and committed intern. I was so confident that I would get this residency that I made arrangements to swap a house with Dr. Alvin Loving, a University of Michigan professor who had recently received an appointment with the City of Detroit. The agreement was that I would stay in his home during my residency and that he would stay in my home in Detroit during the term of his appointment in that city.

Despite my confidence and my plans, it was not to be. It troubled me considerably that I was not accepted at FOH, not only because I performed well as an intern, but I had been befriended by staff physicians, two of whom had even offered to finance my start in practice had I stayed in Flint. I also had strong advocates at Flint Osteopathic, including Jack Stanzler, Allen Corbett, Allen Silverstone, and others. My references did not appear to make a difference and my appeal fell on deaf ears, so I turned to Art Centre Hospital in Detroit.

I had been encouraged to apply for the residency at the Art Centre by my very good friend Charles Murphy, a medical school classmate who was practicing at the hospital. Art Centre was one of several osteopathic hospitals in the Detroit area. At that time, Zieger was the only other osteopathic hospital in Detroit with a Black physician on staff. Art Centre, being the exception, had two Blacks, and it was thought that they were taken because of their relatively small patient volume. The other Black on staff at Art Centre, other than Chuck, was Leo Swainson.

Even though I did not expect to be considered, knowing the history of the hospital, I applied. Chuck was a highly respected physician and his recommendation was not taken lightly. He referred me to Don Ranney, chairman of the Department of Surgery, who later became one of my closest friends.

Dr. Ranney was a very perceptive man and knew immediately that I had a slim chance of getting a residency at Art Centre, first because of my color, but second because of my reputation of being a "troublemaker." My involvement in the Albany Movement was well-known throughout the nation. I had a criminal record, served some time in jail, had an indictment hanging over my head and was to be subjected to a court trial in the not-too-distant future. Needless to say, these things counted against me getting a residency anywhere.

Chuck convinced Ranney to meet me in person before forming an opinion, so I was invited to Detroit. Dr. Ranney reviewed my college transcript and indicated that he wanted me as a resident, but that if he submitted my name cold to the House Staff Training Committee, I would never pass. He felt it was necessary for members of the committee to get to know me personally if I were to have any chance at all at the residency. He recommended that I sign on as a house physician for a year, and he would schedule my work hours so

The Move Back North

that I could start at midnight and work until noon. That way he could assign me to assist in surgery during the morning hours.

This arrangement afforded me a valuable opportunity to be exposed to most of the staff physicians as well as administration. A.C. Johnson, D.O., founder of Art Centre Hospital, was the medical director and the hospital's ultimate authority—an authority that was not questioned by anyone. He virtually handpicked the staff and board members. After several months serving as a house physician and assisting in surgery, Dr. Ranney thought that it was time for me to meet Dr. Johnson, who by this time was aware of my background and my performance at Art Centre.

Don Ranney had become a great friend. He would provide wise counsel and guidance, chastise me when I needed it, and throw his arms around me and protect me against those who were not supportive of my being at Art Centre. Ranney advised me on how I should connect with Dr. Johnson. He indicated that though Dr. Johnson accepted me, it was not necessarily his choice, but that he was also a realist. Dr. Johnson thought that the time had come to begin to break down the racial barriers that existed in Art Centre Hospital. He had certain reservations about my civil rights activities, yet he was confident that I had the intellectual background that was sufficient to be a surgical resident.

Ranney advised that at no time should I discuss business with Dr. Johnson after lunch. There was a tendency for executives to have two-martini lunches. This was common throughout the business world at the time. As a matter of fact, many of the businessmen, recognizing the fact that not all would have a two-martini lunch, wanted to keep up the average and would have four or more martinis. The after-lunch condition of Dr. Johnson was not conducive to important business discussions.

I was quite apprehensive about meeting Dr. Johnson, as he was not an overly warm person. His reputation was that of an excellent surgeon who was practically self-taught, and as a successful businessman who was able to own and operate a hospital. He had few interests outside of these two areas.

I was invited into Dr. Johnson's private office, where he greeted me rather coldly and stated, "I'm aware of what you've done in school and as an intern, so I know that you have what it takes to become a surgical resident. What I want to know is, if we take you as a resident, would you have a demonstration at this hospital?"

I had to smile, for this was the last thing I had expected, and replied "I hope that I would never have the necessity of demonstrating at this hospital." I went on to say, "I am here to learn to be a surgeon, and I understand that I can get the best possible training here with you."

This seemed to satisfy Dr. Johnson, for I was soon notified that I was given a position as a surgical resident at Art Centre, the first Black to receive such an appointment at any hospital in Detroit. (Mt. Clemens General, an osteopathic hospital in a suburb in Detroit, was the first osteopathic hospital to have a Black surgical resident anywhere. Cliff Isaac completed a surgical residency in the mid-1960s and then developed a very successful surgical practice there.)

I was very excited about being accepted as a resident at Art Centre Hospital, for it afforded me the opportunity to work with one of the most highly respected surgeons in the osteopathic profession. Dr. Johnson had the reputation of being a skilled and knowledgeable surgeon. He was versatile in that there was no surgery known that he could not do nor had not done, including open heart and neurosurgery. During his era of practice, which extended for more than 40 years, there were few sub-specialists, and practically none operating in small community hospitals. The Art Centre Hospital housed more than 160 beds, which were always filled. It was also a major training institution for osteopathic interns and residents, primarily in surgery and internal medicine.

Three of Dr. Johnson's graduate residents stayed and formed the Art Centre Clinical Group. While none of the three had subspecialty training, Dr. Johnson designated Dale Christman as the orthopod,

The Move Back North

Don Welch as the urologist, and Don Ranney as the general surgeon. This was the beginning of subspecialty surgical practice at Art Centre, if not subspecialty training.

While Dr. Christman and Dr. Welch were very competent surgeons, they did not begin to approach Don Ranney when it came to didactics and introducing new operative procedures. Don was widely read, and did not limit his surgical practice to what was usual and customary for general surgeons. Ranney was very innovative and when he needed medical equipment that was not readily available, he would design and build it: for example, he created the first negative pressure apparatus that was used following thoracic surgery. He also invented an apparatus for injecting radio-opaque material into the lymphatic system. Though Ranney limited himself in neurosurgery, he did not hesitate to do any other kind of surgery, perhaps because of his exposure to the fearless innovation of A.C. Johnson, who was perhaps among the most versatile and skilled surgeons of his day.

Ranney dabbled in urology and was quite competent at operations on the kidney, ureters, and bladder; however, he never quite mastered the trans-urethral section of the prostate (TURP). It is understandable when you consider the TURP was performed through a resectoscope that utilized an incandescent lamp that probably had no more than fifteen watts of light power. Later, once the fiber optic resectoscope was introduced, it was like opening up a whole new world of trans-urethral surgery.

Don Welch also did a variety of surgical procedures but was focused on developing his skills as a urological surgeon, and it was he who gave me my first exposure to TURP.

Dale Christman was an excellent technician, and one in whom you could have absolute confidence in following the dictum of the founder of osteopathic medicine, Andrew Taylor Still, i.e., "First of all, do no harm." Dr. Christman learned most of his orthopedics from the textbooks that he regularly devoured. He often said that reading a textbook on orthopedic surgery to him was like reading *Ladies' Home Journal* in that it was informative and entertaining.

I rarely got to operate with the master, A.C. Johnson, as he was in his declining years during my residency, but there would be the occasional referring physician who would insist on Dr. Johnson performing the operation on their patients.

My year as a house physician and three years as a resident went by rapidly, and upon completion of my training, I was invited to join the surgical group of Christman, Ranney, and Welch. This was a great honor. To be invited to join your trainers was something that I could never have envisioned. They had at least as much, if not more, confidence in my future success as a surgeon as I did.

The Making of a Felon

While my years in surgical training were uneventful, I cannot say that they were without their periods of doubt and uncertainty. When I started my residency, I had a federal indictment outstanding, and it was just a matter of time before my case would come up for trial. The U.S. Attorney in Georgia scheduled the case for trial in the court of Judge Elliott in Albany. The same judge who had apparently purposefully absented himself from his office to avoid a petition to set aside the injunction against us demonstrating. Needless to say, I did not relish the idea of going into Judge Elliott's court, but I was left with no choice.

I returned to Albany for trial. I had been accused of obstruction of justice, which was tantamount to attempting to overthrow the government. I could state with no equivocation that was the intent, for we felt segregation laws of the state of Georgia were unconstitutional, and the only way that we could change the law was to test it in a court of law.

Several days in Federal District Court in Albany resulted in a hung jury. I later discovered that in this all-White jury, there was someone who would not vote for conviction because he knew I was not a criminal; I was demonstrating for a just cause.

At the end of the trial, the prosecuting attorney indicated that he would bring the case back to trial again, which was his prerogative. This also meant that I had more months of apprehension relative to my ultimate fate in the federal courts, having been charged with such a serious felony.

I returned to Detroit and, although exhausted, resumed my studies as a surgical resident. Months later I was notified that my case was rescheduled for trial. I proceeded to contact attorney George Crockett Jr., who had, on numerous occasions, represented civil rights activists in the South without charge. Attorney Crockett was one of the most highly respected lawyers in Detroit and was well-known nationally as a civil rights activist and a constitutional lawyer.

Two events occurred about this same time that caused me further apprehension and concern. First, I had been contacted by the local Internal Revenue Service advising me that I was under investigation for not having filed income tax for several years while practicing in Albany. IRS agents came to my home to serve papers, only to discover that I had documents, including income tax returns and canceled checks verifying that I had in fact never failed to file income tax. It is coincidental that the agents were Black and indicated with a sigh of relief that they were very happy that I had kept these documents because someone in Georgia was out to get me.

The next event was when the U.S. Marshals came to my home to arrest me, and to place me in jail where I was to stay until my trial for the federal indictment. Since, at the time, I was in the hospital following a minor surgical procedure, the U.S. Marshals got as much information as they could from my wife and left. Norma promptly called our lawyer, Clarence Lassiter, who told her he did not want to alarm her, but that the U.S. Marshals could go into the hospital and take me out of bed to arrest me.

Fortunately, that did not occur. A sympathetic U.S. Marshal called my wife and told her to have me contact him when I was released

The Making of a Felon

from the hospital. When I got home, I called the Marshal and he said, "You are to come to the Federal Building to be placed under arrest, but do not come until a judge is sitting on the bench so we can immediately take you from the jail to the judge's chambers where you will possibly be able to be released on bond."

I contacted Attorney Crockett. He was familiar with the charges filed against me as he was constantly in touch with Legal Aid, the Defense Fund of the NAACP, and other civil rights lawyers. Crockett asked that I come to his house the following evening after dark. There was someone he wanted me to meet. Little did I know the person he wanted me to meet was a federal court judge. He did not know which federal judge would be assigned my case, but he wanted to make certain that at least one of the federal court judges was familiar with the circumstances surrounding my indictment.

When I met with Attorney Crockett and this judge, I began to explain the circumstances surrounding my arrest, my indictment, and my trial in Georgia. The judge promptly stopped me and said, "I know you, all about you, what you were doing, why you were arrested, and what happened in your first trial. I know all of this because my wife's nephew was in jail with you and he wrote a very vivid and detailed account of his experiences in the Albany Movement. I was so impressed that I submitted his writings to the Harvard Review for publication, with the stipulation that they be printed just as written. Harvard Review declined to publish the unedited writings, and I refused to let them publish it otherwise."

I was somewhat relieved that at least there was a Federal District Court judge who was aware of the circumstances surrounding my arrest and indictment and subsequent trial. I also knew that it was a criminal offense to attempt to influence a judge in any case outside of the courtroom. I was grateful that I did not have to tell the judge anything because he was very familiar with the Albany Movement and with my involvement personally.

I followed the instructions of the U.S. Marshal who had advised me to call before submitting myself for arrest. When I did present at the U.S. Marshal's Office in the Federal Court Building, I was promptly handcuffed and taken to a jail cell. I asked, of course, about the necessity for the handcuffs when I had voluntarily turned myself in. I was told this was the standard operating procedure. I did not stay in the jail cell long before the Marshal took me to the courtroom. Of course, I had hoped that the judge would be the same person with whom I had met informally. To my surprise and renewed apprehension, it was not; in front of me was Judge Theodore Levin, the chief judge of this district.

As I was seated in the courtroom they removed the handcuffs. I turned to the Marshal and said, "I need to go to the men's room." He said, "OK. Go out the door, turn to your left, and it's the third door on the right."

I asked, "Don't you want to put the handcuffs back on?" He replied, "Oh, no. Not necessary."

This was rather confusing in that although I had voluntarily surrendered, I had been placed in handcuffs, locked in a cell, transported to the courtroom in handcuffs. The handcuffs were removed, and I was permitted to leave the courtroom unescorted to go to the men's room, expected to return. Well, I did return, where I would face Judge Levin.

My lawyer, George Crockett, and the U.S. District Attorney made opening statements. The judge replied abruptly, "I know as much about this case as I want to know, and I'm ready to pronounce sentence."

I spoke up and said, "Your Honor, I have not had the opportunity to make a statement."

The judge again said, "I know as much about this case as I want to know, and I am ready to pronounce sentence." He looked directly at me.

"I sentence you to 20 in the federal penitentiary."

There was a silence that seemed like an eternity, and I must have died a thousand deaths. The pause was only a matter of a few seconds in which the judge drew a breath to say, "However, I will

The Making of a Felon

suspend that sentence and place you on probation for a year without supervision. Case closed."

It was as though I had received an electric shock and was brought back to life. My heart had stopped. I was frozen somewhere in time and space until I heard those words "on probation without supervision." My lawyer and I looked at each other as he said, "Thank you, your Honor."

The U.S. Attorney promptly left, and my attorney and I followed the probation officer to his office off the courtroom. Attorney Crockett asked the probation officer, "What does probation without supervision mean, exactly?"

The probation officer said, "I don't know. I've never had a case of probation without any supervision. So far as I know, it means you do not have to report. Just don't get into any kind of trouble for a year."

We left the court relieved that no indictment was held over my head. However, from that day on, I had to live my life as a convicted felon. This would become a part of my permanent record, and I feared that one day it might have an effect on my ability to continue as a resident and to regain my license to practice medicine and surgery.

Needless to say, during the ensuing year, I did not receive even a parking ticket. I was very careful to abide by the ruling of the court that I would stay on probation for a year. I did not want Judge Levin to have the occasion to have me in court faced with any criminal charges, no matter how minor they may be. I completed the year without incident and went on to complete my residency in general surgery.

Civil Rights in Detroit
1967–1975

After residency, I joined the group of Ranney, Christman, and Welch after some negotiations. Once an agreement was reached on my salary, I asked for one month's vacation with pay in advance. That stunned a couple of members of the group. However, Ranney insisted that I take time off. I had been at Art Centre as a house physician and a resident for four years and he anticipated that I would be very busy in practice. He agreed that I needed time for myself and for my family.

I was advanced $2,000, and for the first time in four years, I took the family on vacation to Disneyland in Anaheim, California. We had a glorious time on the rides and even played golf on a putt-putt course. It was the best vacation we had had in many years. As a matter of fact, it was the only vacation we had had in four years.

I returned from Disneyland refreshed and eager to start into practice. My patient load immediately increased until I was as busy as I could possibly be. My surgical privileges had been granted by Mahlon Ponitz, D.O., who had retired from the practice of anesthesiology to become the medical director of Art Centre. My privileges read "granted privileges as conscience dictates." This meant that my privileges were virtually unlimited. I had demonstrated a level of skill and integrity during my residency that would govern what surgical procedures I would perform in practice. Of course, such open-ended privileges would not be considered adequate in today's litigious society. My privileges later became more restricted with the advent of peer review and government intervention.

My practice was not limited to just Black patients. Soon, I had as many, if not more, White patients. I came to the conclusion that patients had confidence in their family physician. They trusted the judgment of their family physician and were confident that a referral would not be made to a specialist who was not well-qualified.

After entering practice and having established a good referral base, I began to get involved in community affairs. I had joined New Light Baptist Church, whose pastor was the Rev. Cornell E. Talley, a close friend of Martin Luther King, Jr. King had recommended New Light as a church where he thought I would be most at home. Rev. Talley had recently moved to Detroit and was replacing a pastor of many years, the Rev. Anderson Major Martin, father of Miriam Martin, who married one of my colleagues, Frank Clark, D.O.

The Rev. Talley had a huge following and he preached to a church filled to capacity at least twice every Sunday. His choirs were outstanding, and Talley was among the most captivating preachers that I had ever heard. He was characterized as a Bible preacher. On many occasions I would go to church on Sunday morning after having been on duty at the hospital all night, with the intent perhaps of taking a nap during the sermon, only to be aroused and awakened by a story being told by Rev. Talley. He had the ability to paint a picture in words, and I could not wait to have him finish the masterpiece. No one could tell a Bible story better. He and I became more than just pastor and member; we became very good friends.

Ultimately, I was saddened that we were forced to make the decision to leave New Light Church. The Rev. Talley, like many other pastors in Detroit, withdrew his support from Dr. King because of his vocal opposition to the United States' involvement in Vietnam. I

Civil Rights in Detroit

could not, in good conscience, remain in a church that did not support King, but I remained friends with Talley and his family for many years after we left New Light.

I was also a volunteer member of the Highland Park YMCA Board of Directors. I had frequented the Y as a member for several years, as I found it convenient to stop there on my way home from the hospital. I would go to exercise and to swim and occasionally to try my hand at racquetball. I never became very good at racquetball, but I did manage to stay in good physical condition through my other exercise activities.

After several years as a member of the board, I was asked to chair the 125th anniversary celebration of the Metropolitan YMCA. I willingly accepted the responsibility and proceeded to put together a program. I was able to secure the services of Lou Gossett, the Emmy- and Oscar-winning actor, and I was able to get Andrew Young, then ambassador to the United Nations, to be the keynote speaker.

We secured the Riverview Ballroom at Cobo Hall, which was the largest room in the convention center. There was a commitment made for several hundred tickets, but as the date approached, only a few tickets had been sold. William Cruse, executive director of the YMCA, called a meeting of the board of directors with the anniversary committee. He announced that ticket sales were lower than anticipated; we had paid to reserve the room at Cobo Hall and had guaranteed hundreds of dinners. He was concerned over the potential for failure of the event, and the significant loss of money for the YMCA. Cruse turned to me and asked, "What do you do in a crisis situation like this?"

I said, "I can tell you what we did in Georgia at the height of the Albany Movement when things were not going well."

He pleaded, "Whatever it was that you did then, we need it now."

I said, "We will all stand, hold hands, and sing 'We Shall Overcome.'"

All of the directors and members of the anniversary committee stood, held hands, and sang. It seemed to last an eternity, but when we were done, confidence had been restored and everyone felt that the event would still be a success.

The tickets were sold. The air was filled with excitement, not only for the YMCA's 125th anniversary, but it was the first time the people of Detroit would have the opportunity to see the U.N. Ambassador.

On the day of the event, early in the morning, I was in the midst of a busy surgical schedule when I received a phone call from Stoney Cook, Andy Young's chief of staff.

He said, "Andy Young will not be able to attend the YMCA celebration. He is a member of the Security Council, which has been called into an emergency session."

Upon hearing this, I dropped the phone, leaned against the wall, and slid onto the floor, where I sat motionless for several minutes. I felt the blood drain from my body as I sat for what appeared to be a long, long time. Thoughts raced through my mind about what I would tell hundreds of people who had paid thousands of dollars to see and hear the U.N. ambassador. How would I explain to Lou Gossett, who flew in from Los Angeles to be the master of ceremonies, that we would have no keynote speaker? How would I explain to members and supporters of the YMCA that I had failed as chairman of this anniversary celebration?

The doctors and nurses in the operating suite came to my aid, as they thought I was physically ill, until I explained that this was not a physical but an emotional illness that was having the same effect on my body. They all began to make suggestions as to how I might remedy the situation.

Earle Spohn offered to call a friend who was an officer in a major corporation who might have a private plane in the event that the Security Council session ended in time for Young to make it. I asked Spohn to make the call and to have his contact ready in the event he was needed. I don't know how, but I managed to finish my surgical schedule and left early for Cobo Hall, maintaining constant contact with Cook at the U.N. The event was scheduled to start at 6 p.m. and at 3 p.m. Andy Young was leaving the UN Security Council. Cook

Civil Rights in Detroit

already canceled the reservation they had made, and all other flights from New York to Detroit were filled.

Soon after three o'clock, I received a call from Cook. Andy Young was free to come to Detroit, but he could not get an airplane reservation. Another member of the YMCA board knew an official from a major airline. He offered his services, which I readily accepted, and a call was placed. I called Cook and told him that arrangements were being made for Young to be on the next commercial airline flight from New York getting him into Detroit by 7:30 pm. He agreed to start for LaGuardia Airport immediately. I later learned that when he arrived at the ticket counter, there were several very irate first-class passengers who had been bumped to accommodate the U.N. ambassador and his entourage.

Cobo Hall Riverview Ballroom was filled to capacity, Lou Gossett was holding the audience spellbound, and we were all awaiting the arrival of Andy Young. It was after dinner and approaching eight o'clock when our keynote finally arrived at the event, much to the relief of myself, the hundreds who had come, and most especially the board members of the YMCA.

It was my turn to introduce Andy, and I started with, "The only person who would know what I have gone through this day is the person who does my laundry." The crowd reacted with a loud roar of laughter. They were thrilled with having the opportunity to hear from the ambassador. After a brief introduction, Andy, in his own inimitable way, gave a moving and dramatic speech that was fitting for the anniversary of this long-standing American institution. The celebration was a success, and I was again in the good graces of the Metropolitan YMCA.

Freedom Redefined

After we left Albany, I stayed in almost constant contact with Martin Luther King, Jr. We frequently would contact each other by telephone or by letter, and I would often locate him in some remote part of Alabama or Mississippi. He found, much to my regret, his foundation of support crumbling beneath him, even those who had marched side-by-side with him from the early days of the Civil Rights Movement in Montgomery, Alabama. The issue was his public criticism of the United States' involvement in the Vietnam War.

Martin had taken the position that the war in Vietnam was not justified and was immoral. While he did not openly preach defiance or encourage young men to avoid the draft, he certainly did not encourage participation in this police action that was never declared a war.

Martin had become accustomed to criticism for his activities, and there were frequent occasions when his motivation and his tactics were not understood, even by those who considered themselves his strongest supporters. This frequent criticism prompted Martin to pen a very detailed and poignant letter from the jail in

Birmingham that proved to be one of his classic writings. Such criticism was also the motive for his writing the book *Why We Can't Wait*.

I was active in civic activities in Detroit in the middle '60s, and had become quite close to my pastor. Cornell Talley was one among a number of pastors in Detroit who publicly denounced Martin from the pulpit, indicating that he would withdraw support from Dr. King until he ceased to criticize the United States' efforts in Vietnam and returned to his civil rights activities in this country.

I was considerably dismayed over this statement and by those of other leading ministers of the city. I knew that they were acting out of their personal concern for the Civil Rights Movement, but also out of a lack of understanding of the reasons behind Martin's criticism.

As a result of my visits to a number of churches in the Detroit area, my familiarity with the pastors, and their awareness of my close relationship with Martin, I was able to call for a meeting between these pastors and Dr. King.

I tracked down Martin in the backwoods of Mississippi, where I was able to reach him by telephone. I indicated that I had a tremendous amount of concern because of the support that he was losing from the leading ministers in the Detroit area. He was, of course, aware of a number of ministers who had never supported him or the Civil Rights Movement. But I told him that I was less concerned about them than I was about those who had been his strongest supporters, including his close personal friend, the Rev. Talley. I urged Martin at his earliest possible convenience to come to Detroit and to attend a meeting that I would arrange.

I set up the meeting at the Park Shelton Hotel, and it was attended by no less than 24 of the leading ministers of the city. Martin came, and he outlined in detail the reasons that he could not support the war effort in Vietnam. Further, he explained why he felt that this war was both unjust and immoral.

He was politely received, but it was not clear that he had a sufficiently convincing argument to persuade the pastors to change their

Freedom Redefined

position until one of the senior ministers, H.H. Coleman, took the floor and spoke on Martin's behalf.

The Rev. Coleman started with, "When I speak from my pulpit on Sunday morning, I am lucky if two or three people in the front row hear and heed my message. When Dr. King speaks, the world listens, for he no longer belongs to just us, the Negroes in America, but he belongs to the world."

A masterful preacher had never been more eloquent. His brief message swayed the group and prompted them to change their position and return their support to Martin and the Civil Rights Movement.

Martin was in Detroit several times, including on June 23, 1963, when he led a march of 125,000 people with his good friend, C.L. Franklin. Later that year he would lead 250,000 people on a march in Washington, D.C., where he gave the greatest and most impressive speech of his career, entitled, "I Have a Dream."

During my surgical residency, I regretted that I was not able to join Dr. King and Rev. Abernathy in the Selma to Montgomery march in 1965. The beginning of this march marked a crucial turning point in the history of the Civil Rights Movement. Never before had Negroes demonstrated the strength of nonviolence and the determination to march on to victory in the face of intimidation, beatings, jailing, and even murder. The eyes of the world were on Selma and on Pettus Bridge. The world saw the punishment being inflicted on innocent people who refused to fight back and who were willing to sacrifice their bodies in their quest.

After completing my residency, I began to become more active in civil rights, especially within the Southern Christian Leadership Conference. Dr. King had invited me to become a member of the SCLC board, and of course, I accepted. I felt somewhat out of place in that the majority of the board members were preachers and pastors of large, well-established, prestigious churches. One can only imagine how spirited the meetings were with a group of 20 preachers, all of whom were head of their congregations and were rarely challenged on their decisions. Daddy King, Martin's father, and my stepfather-in-law, were notorious for engaging in very heated debates. There was a strong love/hate relationship between these two. I cannot imagine anyone taking more joy out of those debates than Daddy King and Roland Smith.

An Unfathomable Loss

Martin and I maintained close ties after I left Georgia. Norma, our children, and I always looked forward to his visits, for our home in Detroit was always on his agenda. He and Abernathy especially enjoyed Norma's cooking, and she delighted in preparing their favorite meals. Abernathy was the godfather of our oldest daughter, Laurita, and Martin's youngest daughter, Yolanda, who was later a classmate of our youngest, Dee-Dee.

On the afternoon of April 4, 1968, when I was on the telephone speaking to Coretta Scott King, trying to get in touch with Martin to invite him to an event in Detroit, our conversation was abruptly interrupted when Coretta said, "Excuse me, Andy, somebody is on the other phone, and it's something about Martin." She left the phone, never to return.

The television was on, and news flashed over the air that Martin Luther King Jr. had been assassinated in Memphis, Tennessee. I was shocked and called my family together to watch the news that was now being spread all over the world. I had not smoked for several years and rarely drank an alcoholic beverage, but I do believe that night I never left the television, smoking and drinking while I tried to cope with the loss of one who had become a dear personal friend, and a friend of freedom-loving people the world over. There was no comfort to be found, for almost immediately, news flashed about riots breaking out in various cities throughout the United States. The death of Martin marked the end of an era.

The next few days were filled with news about the murder and, of course, of Martin's life and his legacy. There was also much about the

Freedom Redefined

search for his assassin, and there were conspiracy theories that had led to the killing. The King family and SCLC were in preparation for an appropriate funeral that would be held at the historic Ebenezer Baptist Church, where he was pastor. People from all walks of life—prominent politicians and dignitaries, world leaders—were all making preparations to attend the funeral in Atlanta. The Civil Rights Movement seemed to be in a state of suspended animation, or in its negative, as many abandoned the principles of nonviolence and resorted to rioting.

Thousands of people descended on Atlanta for the funeral and those of us who were SCLC board members were assigned front-row seats. However, in the spirit of the Civil Rights Movement, board members relinquished their seats for visiting dignitaries, including the president of the United States, Cabinet members, and visiting members of Congress. The SCLC board members observed the funeral via television, first from the Wheat Street Baptist Church and later from an administration building on the campus of Morehouse College. Ironically, SCLC board members, among those closest to Martin in life, never got close to Ebenezer Church nor to the gravesite in Lincoln Cemetery.

The loss of Martin Luther King Jr. has been felt around the world. Never before in history had one so inspired so many people yearning to be free, to challenge a racist society and do it with love and nonviolence. It is not likely that this generation will produce another leader who can equal his impact on society.

Growing as a Surgeon and a Leader
1967–1984

A.C. Johnson, who had founded Art Centre Hospital and had been almost single-handedly responsible for making it one of the major training institutions in the osteopathic profession, had finally died in defiance. He was completely in charge of his life until he was ready to give it up. During his last illness, he did not assume the role of being dependent very well. As a matter of fact, one morning as I was visiting him, he awakened as I entered the room and loudly announced, "I am not dead yet!" I felt as though he was looking forward to death since he could no longer be in control of his life. He died soon thereafter, but I will never forget the privilege I had of working with one of the most premier osteopathic surgeons.

It was in the early 1970s that I elected to leave Art Centre, where I had practiced since I completed my residency in 1967. The original Art Centre clinical group had begun to disintegrate as Don Welch left for warmer climates in Phoenix, a rapidly growing area with a need for his skills. We had been moved out of the Park Sheraton Hotel, where we had our offices and relocated to Woodward Avenue near Seven Mile. We renamed ourselves RANCHAND, for Ranney, Christman, and Anderson. We were incorporated by the then-practicing attorneys John Feikens, who later became a United States District Court Judge, and Robert Dice. We practiced together for several years until Ranney was invited to join Welch in Phoenix, as there was an increased need for more urological surgeons at Phoenix General Hospital. This left me alone with Dale Christman, who was a fine orthopedic surgeon but had no desire to be involved in managing an office. I therefore elected to dissolve our group, and I joined the Zieger Clinical Group, which they jokingly referred to as the "Zieger Criminal Group."

Dr. Allen Zieger was founder of the Zieger Osteopathic Hospital and head of the clinical group, offering hospital privileges to both Jewish and Black physicians at a time when there were limited opportunities. He did no surgery during the years I was a part of the group, yet he continued on the payroll. This arrangement was not too uncommon in hospitals that had been built by surgeons. Dr. Zieger was a man of vision and a very astute businessman. He early sensed the shifting of the population from the inner city of Detroit to the suburbs and found land northwest of the intersection of Eight Mile Road and Grand River. He then proceeded to build a new hospital, Botsford General, which would become the suburban outreach of the Zieger Hospital Corporation. It later became the primary hospital for the corporation when Zieger Osteopathic Hospital merged with Art Centre Hospital to form the Michigan Osteopathic Medical Center.

Surgeons, obstetricians-gynecologists, and family practitioners comprised the group. At the time I entered practice with them, I was enamored with the opportunity to work with such notable and highly respected surgeons as Ellis Siefer, Louis Spagnuolo, Harris Mainster, and Anthony Messana.

Dr. Siefer was the senior member of the surgical group and was an outstanding surgeon and teacher. I learned much about surgery from him, and he was a constant source of encouragement. A very versatile surgeon who was as comfortable doing gynecologic surgery as he was gastrointestinal or urological surgery, he was quite skilled technically.

Dr. Spagnuolo had been Siefer's partner since he entered practice. Very well-liked by all staff physicians, residents, interns, medical students, and patients, Spagnuolo was not as aggressive and entrepreneurial as Zieger but was certainly a very competent surgeon for the procedures he performed.

Dr. Mainster was the highest-producing surgeon in the group, as he always seemed to be full of energy. He worked long hours, took very good care of his referring doctors, and was a very competent surgeon. Mainster must have thought he was somewhat limited being a member of the Zieger Clinical Group and therefore branched out on his own and established a very successful practice at Botsford General Hospital. This was possibly as much for financial reasons as any other, for certainly he was compatible with other members of the group and had a great deal of respect for Drs. Siefer and Spagnuolo.

Dr. Messana had potential that was rarely challenged or explored. While a very capable surgeon, he did not always appear to have the ambition or the drive to do more than was necessary to maintain his position in the group. Messana's abilities were most evident during a period when he was in practice alone. During that time, he worked long hours and was very dependable. These were traits that were not always evident when he was a part of the group.

The Zieger Clinical Group gradually disintegrated once Mainster established a solo practice, and Siefer and Spagnuolo began to do more and more of their work at Botsford Hospital. Sensing the lack of progress at Zieger directly related to the growth of Botsford, I elected to establish my own surgical group.

I returned to Art Centre Hospital where I had trained and now started a solo practice of surgery. I was soon joined by Randolphe Roulier, a well-established surgeon who had come on staff at the Centre in the early 1970s before Ranney left for Arizona. Dr. Roulier was a very aggressive surgeon who was also very ambitious. He had been trained at Detroit Osteopathic Hospital, the premiere educational institution in the profession. After his residency, he began a solo practice that grew rapidly, as the principal surgeon at a small, 50-bed hospital, he expanded his practice to include Detroit Osteopathic and Art Centre Hospitals.

Roulier was seeking a partner to start a group practice, and therefore he and I joined forces to form the Detroit Surgical Associates. We were later joined by Earle Spohn and Anthony Messana. There were now four of us in a group surgical practice operating out of several hospitals in the Detroit metropolitan area.

Spohn had also trained at Detroit Osteopathic Hospital and had developed a small but loyal group of followers who were his referring doctors. He was very likable and always had a friendly smile and cordial manner. Patients tended to like Spohn, and he got along well with his colleagues.

Detroit Surgical Associates eventually took in a fifth member, William Gilchrist Anderson II, who was an obstetrician-gynecologist, recently graduated from the residency program at Bi-County Community Hospital. Gil was well-trained and a very skilled obstetrician and gynecologic surgeon. I found great joy in operating with Gil as a father-son surgical team.

Gil stayed in the group only a few years, just long enough to learn how to operate a practice and to get the names, addresses, and phone numbers of the patients that he wanted to continue to care for in solo practice as an obstetrician-gynecologist. The conditions under which Gil left the group angered some of my partners; however, I indicated that we must have done something right in training Gil. He had become not only a well-qualified and highly respected physician but also demonstrated that he had acquired some business acumen. I was very proud of his decision to test his wings in solo practice. This proved to be a very wise move on his part, as he was able to cover us in much of our general surgical practice, yet we could not cover him in the practice of obstetrics. He was later joined by Brent Gillum to form another group practice that endured for many years.

Growing as a Surgeon and a Leader

Prior to 1970, most osteopathic physicians had privileges to admit and treat their patients at one or more osteopathic hospitals. It was considered a necessity in practice. Family physicians were given the privilege of managing patient care to the extent of their ability and experience. Many family practitioners managed uncomplicated medical problems and performed many minor surgical procedures. They only referred cases that exceeded their scope of training.

Gaining hospital privileges was at a premium at some hospitals, which charged attending physicians a "bed tax," an amount paid to the hospital by the physician for the privilege of admitting and treating patients. It is ironic that that practice fell into disfavor as more and more hospitals opened their doors to osteopathic physicians.

The hospital staff organization served both as the training ground and the springboard to enter the politics of the profession at the county, state, and ultimately, at the national level. The professional staffs were well organized by departments and there were officers of the entire staff. I was privileged after a few years to serve as chairman of the Department of Surgery and later chief of staff.

It ultimately became evident to the boards and administrations of several small osteopathic hospitals that the era of institutions with fewer than 200 beds was rapidly coming to an end. Small community hospitals simply could not afford the latest, up-to-date, sophisticated medical technology. They began to look at opportunities to merge several of the small hospitals into a larger one that would be able to provide all of the services reasonably expected of a hospital in a metropolitan area.

The Osteopathic Hospital Development Corporation was initially formed with representatives from Art Centre, Zieger, and Detroit Osteopathic. Northwest General Hospital was invited to join the group but declined. There were many meetings over many months during the mid-1970s, and one by one, hospitals dropped out of the Development Corporation for a variety of reasons, not the least of which was a desire to remain autonomous, either as a hospital or as a department within one of the existing hospitals. Much of the advantage of a merger would have been lost if the merged hospitals had to maintain a separate department for each of the specialties represented in each of the hospitals. Ultimately, Zieger and Art Centre were named in the Osteopathic Hospital Development Corporation, which later became the Osteopathic Hospital of Detroit, Inc. (OHDI).

I was first a board member and later chairman of the board of OHDI, and with the organization of OHDI, I again became its chairman. Robert Wildish, administrator, later named president, represented Art Centre Hospital along with several of the hospital board members. Gershon Cooper, administrator and later president of the Zieger Osteopathic Hospital Corporation, and a few of its board members were representatives of the Zieger Osteopathic Hospital. OHDI then began to develop plans for building a new hospital to replace Zieger and Art Centre Hospitals.

Things did not always go smoothly in merging the two hospital corporations and building a new hospital. Northwest General Hospital was still independent, and because of its small size and limited capacity, was in jeopardy of closing unless it aligned itself with a bigger hospital. The Zieger Osteopathic Hospital Corporation entered into discussions with Northwest General, exploring opportunities for an acquisition. This appeared to be a direct conflict of interest in that the Zieger Osteopathic Hospital Corporation had representatives on the board of OHDI but also wanted Northwest General to be a part of the merged hospitals. This apparent conflict led to the resignation of representatives from the Zieger Osteopathic Hospital Corporation from the OHDI board, but the development of the new hospital continued.

It was in 1980 that the new osteopathic hospital was preparing to open under the name of the Michigan Osteopathic Medical Center, often referred to as MOMC. Robert Wildish soon announced his retirement at the age of 55, stating that this had been his long-range plan. The newly formed board of OHDI reluctantly accepted his resignation, but at the same time elected to retire Mahlon Ponitz, who had been the medical director. Dr. Ponitz was somewhat reluctant to retire in that he had planned on continuing for several years. However, it was the desire of the board to make a clean sweep at the top and to bring in a new president/chief executive officer and chief medical officer.

Based on Bob Wildish's recommendation, the board elected to appoint the man who had been the chief financial officer throughout his administration to be the new president and chief executive officer. Bob had often said that he could not have been nearly as effective if it had not been for this man, and there was no doubt that he was a whiz with figures. Yet he was somewhat lacking in his ability to win over and influence people; his personality was quite different from Bob's.

I was then asked to consider resigning as chairman of the board and assuming the position of chief medical officer. I readily accepted the offer because I felt as though I could be of greatest value to the newly formed hospital corporation in that post.

At Art Centre, there was an administrative director of medical education who possessed extraordinary skills in planning for hospital functions and hospital travel, both for professional meetings and for recruitment. Cost was no object, and I must confess, most of us were not cost-conscious. Chuck Yonka was loved by all, especially members of the hospital auxiliary, whom he took care of very well as he planned many of their activities. It is unfortunate that Chuck Yonka met an untimely death in an automobile accident soon after the new president and chief executive officer had been selected. This was a sad time for the many who loved Chuck, and I am not certain that the administration was sufficiently sensitive to the pain we felt with his loss.

My good friend Floyd Meachum had been employed by MOMC as a vice president for medical evaluation, whatever that meant. Bob Wildish had searched for a title for Floyd in that the board had insisted on Bob finding a well-qualified Black hospital officer. The hospital population was predominantly Black, and many of the physicians were Black, but there were no Blacks within the corporation above the level of manager. The hospital board had decreed that there would be no other officers above the level of manager approved until and unless a qualified Black could be found. Thus, Floyd became a vice president.

This was a new era in the practice of medicine and in the operation of our hospitals. We were all beginning to feel the pressures of outside influences on hospital utilization and charges. Most of us had become accustomed to a cost-plus reimbursement system and were now being subjected to significant changes in the reimbursement system that required very accurate documentation and justification for all hospital stays and procedures. This was the beginning of the Diagnosis Related Groups (DRG) reimbursement system that was implemented in the mid-1980s, and every hospital was struggling to meet these requirements imposed by this new system. MOMC was not exempt. Therefore, it was incumbent upon me as the chief medical officer to educate the professional staff on how best to manage patient care under this new reimbursement system. I planned many educational programs and constantly monitored the change in practice patterns that would enable the hospital to continue with this new reimbursement system. At the direction of the president, consultants from the University of Michigan were called in at frequent intervals in the advent of the DRG system to evaluate and monitor how MOMC was adapting.

Within six months of the introduction of DRGs, I was called to the office of the president, where I was advised that I had failed to adequately prepare the staff for the new system. I was stunned and taken aback, for I had done an extraordinary amount of work to prepare the staff with a series of lectures, demonstrations and monitoring their activities. The medical staff had adjusted well to the new system.

The president went on to say that the hospital had lost about $20 million, maintaining that it was because of my failure. He insisted that I resign my position as executive vice president/chief medical officer and that I fire my good friend Floyd Meachum, who had been hired as vice president of the hospital corporation. The president went on to tell me that the board had already made the decision to fire me, but out of the goodness of his heart, he would give me the "opportunity" to resign and avoid embarrassment. I told him that I needed time to think about it.

I later discovered that each time the board would go into executive session, when I along with other staff members and members of the administration were asked to leave, the president would have something negative to say about my performance. This had gone on for several months without my knowledge.

I knew deep down in my heart that I could not fire Floyd. He was a friend and, even more importantly, he was doing a superb job. After much gut-wrenching consideration, I declined to fire Floyd and elected to resign.

Following my meeting with the president, I went to the office of Bill Cohan, one of the board members whom I had befriended. Bill and I had traveled extensively throughout the United States for various hospital business meetings. We always found time to get in a little golf together, which we both very much enjoyed, and our wives, Norma and Mary, became good friends, finding things to do while Bill and I were on the links.

Bill told me in no uncertain terms that the board had not given the president those directions. Instead, the president had been told to get with me and work out a plan to address the problems that we had encountered with this new reimbursement program. Bill was not at all inhibited in his reaction to the message that I had brought from the president: He was incensed and expressed it openly. I was immediately convinced that the president had purposely lied to me in his continuing efforts to get me out of the organization. I later discovered that he was very envious of my relationship with the medical staff, employees, and the board and felt threatened by my presence. He thought that I wanted his job.

After my meeting with Bill, I promptly rescinded my resignation, which, of course, had not been accepted by the president and the board of directors.

I filed a court suit for wrongful discharge, naming the president and the entire board. I first went to the Equal Employment Opportunity Commission to file my complaint. While there was much interest shown in my case by the EEOC, I felt as though I needed a private lawyer who specialized in job discrimination. I was referred to the very best by one of the staff lawyers of the EEOC, attorney Laura Mosley.

Susan Winshal, Esq. was head of a very small law firm that specialized in just such cases, and I could not have made a better choice. For the next two years, Sue and I worked together building my case. When I say "we," I mean "we." Sue made me work as hard and as long as she did. Often, we toiled far into the early hours of the morning. She was thorough and detailed and persistent. There were occasions when Norma questioned, "What kind of lawyer kept clients these long hours?"

But the investment of thousands of dollars and months of hard work paid off when we finally got to court. The case was tried in Federal Court with a jury that was very difficult to read. The trial lasted for six weeks and we won with a good judgment. Sue had been magnificent. Her persistence, diligence, and attention to every little detail paid off. But upon questioning the jury after the trial, it was evident that they identified with us and were most impressed with how Sue presented the case. Some on the panel were simply enamored by Sue's attire. She was sharply dressed every day and some said that they could hardly wait until the next session to see what she would be wearing. They also noted my lawyer and me as the only two at the plaintiff's table, while the defendants always brought a team of legal experts, paralegals, and other assistants.

The overriding consideration that was most convincing to the

Growing as a Surgeon and a Leader

jury was the fact that I had been in the hospital corporation for more than 22 years and had held every office possible, and I had only asked that the board meet with me so that I could explain what I was doing for the corporation. The board refused and that, more than anything else, lost the case for them.

Hospital Administration and Education
1986–1991

The trial had been protracted and stressful, most especially for my wife, who was present by my side throughout the six-week ordeal. The jury verdict brought a welcome relief in our lives and the final financial settlement somewhat compensated for the tremendous losses we had suffered during the period of preparation for trial and the trial itself. I was vindicated. Now it was time for me to pick up the pieces, find employment, and prepare for the rest of my professional life. I was yet quite young with no intentions of retiring. I did realize that my career as a surgeon was over, in that it is extremely difficult to stay out of the practice of surgery as long as I had, and to return without going back into residency. I had no intentions of going back into residency.

Chris Allen was administrator of Detroit Osteopathic Hospital. Chris knew of me, and I, of course, had heard of him in that he was the only Black hospital administrator within the osteopathic profession and one of few in the metropolitan Detroit area. Chris called and asked if I would meet with him. I agreed, and he discussed with me the opportunity of employment at DOH in administration. I readily agreed, and he gave me the title of director of governmental affairs.

William G Anderson, DO, FACOS

My duties included active participation in the political affairs impacting the osteopathic profession, especially legislation that would affect the practice of osteopathic medicine at DOH. I was also actively engaged in physician recruiting and evaluating private physicians' practices for possible acquisition by DOH. This position was ideal for me in that it afforded me the opportunity to continue my political activity within the American Osteopathic Association (AOA) and in the state osteopathic association.

In the mid-1980s, DOH was a very busy hospital, providing services that other osteopathic hospitals in Michigan did not—including coronary angiography, open heart surgery, radiation oncology, and invasive radiology. It had a full staff of specialists and super-specialists. In spite of its history and excellent standing in the osteopathic community, it was obvious to us who had been in the institution for several years that there was a rapid decline in the numbers of both the patient and the physician populations. I sensed this, and in discussion with Chris Allen suggested that it would be in the best interest of DOH to seek a partner or an affiliation with a major hospital system.

DOH had dropped out of negotiations with Art Centre and Zieger Hospitals, which had gone on to build a new hospital, Michigan Osteopathic Medical Center (MOMC). The DOH Corporation was now operating three hospitals in the metropolitan area—DOH, Bi-County and Riverside. I recommended that DOH seek affiliation with other hospitals to preserve many of the tertiary services that DOH provided. The board and administration were unable to reach a satisfactory agreement with any area hospitals to preserve these services and, therefore, they were eventually lost.

What remained of DOH was a smaller, yet dedicated, teaching staff with a strong internal medicine group and a seasoned and well-qualified surgeon, Jack Finley. There were also the most progressive radiologists in the profession, whose talents would have been welcomed anywhere—Rick and Joan Taras, a dynamite team, supported by Sylvia England. George Gustafson was chief of radia-

Hospital Administration and Education

tion oncology and had respect in the osteopathic profession. The strong group of internists included Deborah Jo Levan, Dennis Packey, and Arthur Bouier.

DOH was targeted by Detroit-Macomb Hospital Corporation for acquisition. This corporation had built a new hospital, Detroit Riverview, merging Jennings, Blain, and Memorial Hospitals. There was a suburban division, South Macomb, and the corporation was seeking to improve its operations at the inner-city hospital, Detroit Riverview. DOH seemed to be a natural with its strong staff and its history as the premier training institution within the osteopathic profession. This proved to be a very wise move on the part of Detroit Osteopathic Hospital Corporation, for within six months of relocating the DOH operation into Detroit Riverview, there was a significant financial improvement, and for the first time in four years, it showed a positive bottom line.

The turnaround specialist that had been hired by Detroit-Macomb Hospital Corporation to reverse the fortunes of Detroit Riverview was very successful in negotiating the transfer of the DOH staff and services to the Riverview site. Among the very strong attributes of DOH were its educational programs. In addition to students, there were also residents in internal medicine and surgery. Part of the agreement was that the training programs would continue at Detroit Riverview, with the primary training offices being maintained at Bi-County Community Hospital. In this arrangement, the turnaround specialist did not see a place for me in the relocated programs.

Michael Opipari convinced this administrator that it was necessary to have someone in medical education if they were to continue training programs at Riverview. They then reached an agreement that I would be retained as associate director of medical education and that the trainees from Bi-County would be periodically rotated through Riverview Hospital. This was a five-year agreement, subject to termination on one-year notice by either party. This arrangement was satisfactory and served the purposes of DOH and Riverview extremely well. I served as associate DME until the decision had been made by Bi-County that Detroit Riverview Hospital was no longer needed as a training site for students, interns and residents in the Bi-County Programs.

By this time, the Riverview staff had become accustomed to having trainees, and I was approached by several members of the staff, including Mike Woods, chairman of the Department of Surgery; Jack Finley, who was the principal trainer in surgery; Rajindar Sikan, chairman of the Department of Medicine, and Deborah Jo Levan, who was the principal trainer in the Department of Internal Medicine. I indicated that this could be done if certain conditions were made, and if there was sufficient commitment on the part of hospital administration to support these educational programs.

The administration had changed as the turnaround specialist had done his job and was leaving, and Rick Young became the president of Riverview Hospital. With his approval, I began to prepare applications for residencies in obstetrics and gynecology, internal medicine, surgery, family practice, and an internship.

The first residency application that I submitted to the AOA was for OB-GYN. This was a bit out of the ordinary because it was most unusual that a hospital would have a residency program and not have an internship. The OB-GYN residency application was submitted first because MOMC was on the verge of discontinuing its program and had approval for 20 residents. Many of these residents were familiar with Riverview and had served in a moonlighting capacity there. I was able to expedite the application process so that the 20 residents at MOMC would not be displaced, with no alternative program to enter. George Shade, M.D., chairman of the Department of OB-GYN, was very helpful, and in fact, instrumental in getting the program approved. William Stanley, D.O., was retained as the program director, and in a very short period of time, Riverview had approval for a residency program in OB-GYN, and most of the residency slots were filled. The program was started with 18 residents.

In rapid succession, I submitted applications for an internship with 40 positions to be combined with Oakland General Hospital. I

Hospital Administration and Education

also submitted applications for residencies in internal medicine, surgery, and family practice. These were all approved in record time and Detroit Riverview Hospital could boast of having a full complement of third- and fourth-year medical students, interns, and residents for the first time. It is fortuitous that these programs were approved just prior to the enactment of the federal Balanced Budget Act of 1997. This act froze all approved resident positions at the January 1996 level, and all of the resident applications had been approved prior to that cut-off date. Thus, Riverview had the opportunity to fill 66 postgraduate training positions that had not been in existence prior to that time. I consider this among my most satisfying accomplishments during my professional career. It was not because of my genius, but only because I followed the dictum of the right time, the right place, with the right idea.

Climbing the Ladder in the Osteopathic Profession

I was first introduced to the politics of osteopathic medicine as a young man at the invitation of Dr. Raymond A. Gadowski, who was executive director of the Wayne County Osteopathic Association, a local association so large that it outnumbered all but five state associations in the osteopathic profession. Ray, to my knowledge, had been the only executive director of the Wayne County Osteopathic Association, as he had held that position for more than two decades when I was first contacted to become a member of the Wayne County board.

I was as curious as I was ambitious when I accepted Ray's invitation to become involved in county matters. To my knowledge there had never been a Black to serve on the Wayne County Osteopathic Association board of trustees or any other association within the osteopathic profession.

Ray was quite persuasive, and I was easy in that I had the greatest admiration and respect for him as one of the outstanding leaders in the profession. I came to know and love Ray as a close friend. I considered it a privilege to have had the opportunity to learn from him much about the politics of the osteopathic profession. I later got the opportunity to work with him when he was employed by MOMC as the director of medical education.

I had held many staff offices in Art Centre Hospital, so Ray thought I was ready to move on. He coerced me into accepting the position of chairman of the membership committee of the county association. This, I thought, was the least important of all positions that anyone could hold. But it was the stepping stone to the Wayne County board of directors. A year later, I was elected to the board with Ray's support.

Membership in the county association was required for hospital privileges, but attendance at county meetings was not required. As attendance decreased, Ray had a plan to reverse the trend: He would place on the agenda one or two items that would guarantee a good attendance. He would announce a vote on mandatory attendance at county meetings or a vote on an increase in dues. These brought out record-breaking crowds. Later, Ray was elected to the Michigan Osteopathic Association Board of Directors and, in a short period, ascended to the presidency, a well-deserved honor.

I believe that when Ray was elected executive director of Wayne County, it was a "for life" election. He held the position for more than 40 years, up until the time of his death. I succeeded Ray in the post, and it appears as though I will hold the office for life. I only hope that I can contribute as much to the advancement of the profession as did Ray.

Sitting on the American Osteopathic Association board was most revealing, for as a practicing physician, it was difficult for me to understand and appreciate all of the things that go on behind the scenes. It was the AOA that first afforded me the opportunity of becoming an osteopathic physician, of obtaining and protecting my right to practice as an osteopathic physician in all 50 states and many foreign countries. One has to be inside the political arena to have a full appreciation for the efforts that go into maintaining this profession.

It was evident that I was being groomed by the leadership of the

Climbing the Ladder in the Osteopathic Profession

profession to eventually become its president. This grooming required my exposure to every department, every council, every college, every committee, every specialty college, and other component societies of the profession. It was important that I have a working knowledge of all aspects of the AOA, especially in the areas of education, governmental affairs, and administration. I was well prepared, for when I finally ascended to the office of the president, I was quite knowledgeable about the inner workings of the AOA. After having been elected to and serving five successive three-year terms on the board, I was chosen president without apparent dissent.

In retrospect, I acknowledged the fact that it was Frank McDevitt, the osteopathic "godfather," who had strongly supported my political career in the profession. It was Frank who told me several years before it happened, "You will be president of the AOA one day. Be patient and learn all that you can about the profession."

I had selected Atlanta as the site for the House of Delegates meeting in 1994, the year I was inducted as president of the AOA. I chose Atlanta because it was in the state where I was born and where I first entered practice.

Atlanta and Georgia are now vastly different than when I had left there to join the Navy in 1944. Legal segregation and discrimination had become outlawed, and the open practice of segregation and discrimination was relegated to a few isolated cases. There was no open hostility to Blacks, and we were overtly welcomed in all business establishments, including restaurants and hotels.

My inaugural was attended by what seemed to be thousands, who formed an endless line throughout the Grand Marquis Marriott Hotel. Many went through the receiving line and greeted my wife and me. They very politely shook our hands as they were introduced to my biological mother, my civil rights mother, and our five children— Laurita, Gil, Jeannie, Frank, and Dee-Dee. Many would proceed to the end of the line before they would realize that my civil rights mother was, in fact, Rosa Parks. Some of them proceeded to get into the receiving line again in full appreciation of the fact that they were shaking hands with a living legend and a part of the history of America.

At the inaugural luncheon, I was thrilled that my family, led by my wife and with my daughter-in-law Doris and others, had produced a video portraying the major events of my life. My friends said that the master of ceremonies, my son Gil, was exceptionally good and effective. It all seemed to be worth it; that is, whatever sacrifices had been made to obtain this high office in the profession were well warranted.

In my opening remarks, I was pleased to announce that I was most proud that my mother had lived long enough to become "Mrs. Anderson" in Georgia. It was customary that Black females went from "girl" to "auntie" and completely bypassed "Miss" and "Mrs." This was no small thing to both my biological and civil rights mothers to be finally acknowledged as "Mrs."

As president I traveled all over the United States, speaking to all the colleges of osteopathic medicine, to all of the state and component societies, and to all of the specialty colleges. Without exception, I was well received and treated with the respect that is accorded the president of the AOA. I traveled from New York to California, from Washington state to Florida, from Mississippi to Montana, and to all states in between. Some of our state associations were more elaborate in their welcome of the president, but all accorded me the usual courtesies. Some states were exceptional and deserved special mention. The Oklahoma Osteopathic Association, led by its executive director, Bob Jones, was by far the most accommodating of a visiting president. Norma and I have never been treated better. We were met at the airport and escorted by limousine to the Shangri-la Resort, where we were given a suite that was stocked with our favorite beverages, fruit, snacks, and very tasteful gifts. This is not just to say other states did not put forth the efforts, and in all fairness, mention should be made of states like Michigan, Pennsylvania, Georgia, and Florida, that went far beyond expectations in accommodating the visiting president. Even Mississippi, with its small membership, put forth special effort under the leadership of a volunteer executive director, Henry Pace, who was not an osteopathic physician.

The theme for the AOA during my year of presidency was "Osteopathic Medicine—An Idea Whose Time Has Come." There is nothing more powerful than an idea whose time has come, and the time had come for osteopathic medicine. The AOA public relations and communications staff did much to promote this theme, and for that I am deeply grateful.

I served my term out as president of the AOA with a degree of satisfaction, knowing that the profession had advanced a little bit more. During my term of office, I had occasion to make presentations to members of Congress. I also brought together the leadership of the five major medical organizations that were headed by Blacks. It is perhaps coincidental that in the same year of my presidency, the American Medical Association had its first Black president in Lonnie Bristow. The president of the American College of Physicians, Gerald Thomson, was Black. As though three were not enough, the American College of Surgery was moving to elect LaSalle D. Leffall, and Tracey Walton became president of the National Medical Association. For the first time in history, and possibly the only time in this millennium, five major medical groups were all headed by Blacks.

It is also coincidental, and possibly with no relationship one to the other, that Bill Clinton was in his first term as president of the United States, and First Lady Hillary Clinton was gamely trying to overhaul the health care delivery system. In jest, I said that perhaps it was no coincidence that these five major medical groups would be headed by Blacks, because it was anticipated that the Clinton healthcare reform would fail, and the leaders of the medical groups would be blamed for the failure. I said this in jest, but perhaps truer words have not been spoken.

The 1994 AOA convention was held in San Francisco. I had invited the five Black leaders of these major medical groups to be my guests. Bristow and Walton attended and spent a considerable amount of time getting to know more about the osteopathic profession and exploring our concerns related to health care in America.

I invited Andy Young to be the keynote speaker for the convention, and after a direct appeal, he agreed to come at no cost. Andy had completed a stint in the cabinet of President Carter as ambassador to the United Nations and had served two terms as mayor of Atlanta. He was in demand as a speaker all over the world. I considered us to be very fortunate in securing him. He was exceptional and steered the crowd to emotion. He was eloquent, and universally accepted and appreciated across all racial, ethnic, religious, and political party lines. There were ultra-conservative White Republicans who came to me to tell me how much they appreciated his address and felt that they could comfortably vote for him. Needless to say, my stock in the AOA went up considerably!

I had two years of my term remaining on the AOA board when my presidency was over, and it was sort of anticlimactic, for where do you go after you have been president? I think in its wisdom, the AOA keeps its president on the board to take full advantage of the knowledge and experience he or she has gained, not only in the years as president, but also in the many years of service on the board it takes to prepare for the presidency. After completing my two years, I have been asked by nearly every succeeding president to serve on their advisory councils. It is well known that I strongly desire to continue in the politics of the profession until such time as another Black has demonstrated the interest, the commitment, and the ability to take up where I left off.

I was the first Black resident at Art Centre Hospital and later became chairman of the Department of Surgery. I was the first Black to become chief of staff and eventually chairman of the hospital board. I was also the first Black to be certified by the American College of Osteopathic Surgeons.

Being the first in so many of these venues became a burden in that there was a level of expectation that I always had to succeed so other Black osteopathic physicians would have the same opportunities that I had. Being the first was also of considerable concern to me because I did not want to be the only one; I certainly did not want to be the first and last. Wherever I went and whatever positions I held, I was proud of the opportunity given me and did not consider it a successful experience unless a door had been opened for Blacks to follow.

As I write these memoirs, I am so very pleased that other Blacks, like Charles Murphy, Floyd Meachum, Lewin Wyatt, and Barbara Ross-Lee, dotted throughout the profession, have entered into health policy. I hope that they have come to the realization that Blacks get much more being at the table than being outside the door. Also, I have admonished others who have not seen fit to get involved in such roles; they deserve the treatment that they get because of their failure to get involved. I recognize that we all cannot be members of a board, or become president of our organization, but we all can support those who demonstrate a sympathetic understanding of the problems that we, as Black osteopathic physicians, have and are willing to join in our efforts to eliminate all vestiges of segregation and discrimination found throughout the profession.

Get involved through your time, your talent, and your treasure. I'll say it again: *your time, your talent, and your treasure.*

A Rolling Stone
1994–Present

My travels throughout the United States, visiting osteopathic organizations, colleges, schools, and universities and having the opportunity to speak to physician groups, residents, interns, and medical students, continued even after I was no longer president of the AOA. I never declined an invitation to speak because I felt that it was very important that I continue to advance osteopathic medicine.

Paulette Lovell, at Michigan State University College of Osteopathic Medicine, placed me on the regular lecture schedule for the orientation of incoming students. This became custom and continued for decades. To greet the new students and welcome them to the osteopathic profession was an event that I looked forward to each year. I also was called on frequently to speak at student functions at Ohio University College of Osteopathic Medicine, where I was given the Phillips Medal of Public Service. First, the invitations came from Dean Frank Meyers and later, from the new dean, Barbara Ross-Lee, a Robert Wood Johnson Fellow who became the first Black woman to become Dean of a Medical College in the entire United States!

After a number of such visits, Dr. Ross-Lee remarked, "Bill, we can never repay you for all you do for the profession and this college." I replied, "Try, damn it, try. You might surprise yourself." We both got a good laugh out of that exchange, for she knew that I would always willingly accept an invitation to visit and to speak on behalf of osteopathic medicine.

The University of New Jersey School of Osteopathic Medicine for many years extended me an invitation to speak at the White coat ceremony that has now been adopted by more and more colleges of osteopathic medicine. The dean assured a place on my calendar by extending the invitation for the coming year at the close of the ceremony each year. I consider it an honor and a privilege to participate in White coat ceremonies, for it is that time in medical school that students begin to look like doctors, and that makes them act more like doctors. Later, I began to receive invitations to speak at white coat ceremonies for freshman orientation at other colleges of osteopathic medicine across the country.

The Opti Revolution

During my years as president-elect and president of the national American Osteopathic Association (AOA), Mike Opipari and the AOA Council on Postdoctoral Training had developed a revolutionary system of postgraduate training that became known as the OPTI, or Osteopathic Postgraduate Training Institution. I was convinced that this new system was the salvation of our osteopathic training programs, in that many of our small osteopathic hospitals were isolated from academic medical centers and thus could not afford the opportunity for their trainees to get exposed to the latest medical technology.

The objective of the OPTI was to form consortia of osteopathic hospitals and osteopathic colleges to pool resources to more adequately provide training essential for the profession to continue to produce high-quality physicians. I was enthusiastic about the

A Rolling Stone

concept and in my rather extensive travels over a two-year period, I put forth every effort to sell this idea to the osteopathic profession. There was some reluctance and even some resistance in some quarters. However, many osteopathic educators accepted the necessity of such a structure and began to support it. The OPTI concept was finally adopted nationwide and was a model for graduate medical education, improving educational opportunities for osteopathic students, interns and residents.

Helping The Federal Court

Throughout my experiences as a construction laborer, bellhop, bartender, chauffeur, and sometime farmhand, then as a Naval Hospital corpsman, third-string football player, mortician, schoolteacher, singer, disc jockey, radio announcer, family doctor, surgeon, hospital chief medical officer and director of medical education—the last thing that I ever expected to be was a Federal Court-appointed bankruptcy trustee.

When I received the call from the U.S. Attorney's Office requesting that I accept the appointment as a trustee for a hospital in bankruptcy, I was very reluctant. I had limited experience in hospital administration and, of course, no experience as a bankruptcy trustee. The attorney convinced me that they had carefully investigated my background in health care, and they had determined that I was qualified to do the job.

My friend, Chris Allen, had hired me as director of governmental affairs for the Detroit Osteopathic Hospital Corporation, and I was not planning on leaving that position. But when I told him of the appointment as a hospital bankruptcy trustee, he encouraged me to accept it.

There were two other people who had supported my efforts to gain employment after I had left Michigan Health Care Corporation —Tom Caufield, president of Detroit Osteopathic Hospital Corporation, and Mike Opipari, vice president and chief medical officer of the corporation. They both encouraged me to accept the appointment and to do what I could to save the sister hospital. I was also given the assurance that I could take as much time as necessary, and that I would have a job at Detroit Osteopathic Hospital Corporation when it was over. I needed no further encouragement.

I had been a member of the planning committee for the new Southwest Detroit Hospital in the early 1970s. I had been selected to represent Zieger Osteopathic Hospital which had a vested interest in the new hospital. Southwest Detroit Hospital was an outgrowth of the merger of six Black-owned hospitals that had served primarily the Black population of Detroit for nearly a century. Zieger was the only osteopathic hospital included in the merger because it had an obstetrical unit that would be maintained and made available to all staff members.

Southwest Detroit had struggled from the day it opened, burdened by an abundance of uncompensated care and underinsured patients. Many of the Black doctors were in support of the hospital and, for a time, it appeared to flourish. The hopes and ambitions were soon dashed, and the hospital began to collapse under the weight of mounting debt and expenses.

A Rolling Stone

The final blow was dealt as all third-party payers discontinued payments and, in fact, demanded refunds for past overpayments. There was further pressure from the insurance commissioner that required more reserve funds to maintain the health maintenance organization (HMO) that had helped to keep the hospital afloat. Bankruptcy was the only option left, and it really was not an option, as it was forced by creditors.

In retrospect, it would appear as though Southwest Detroit Hospital was doomed to failure from the beginning because of a combination of factors. First, it was built in a remote section of town that was thinly populated and not readily accessible to those most likely to use it. Second, the vast majority of the patients were either uninsured or underinsured, with the principal payer being Medicaid. It did not take long to come to the realization that even the most astute and skilled administrator could not survive in such a reimbursement climate.

Thanks to my very good friend Prince Holliday, I was able to recruit a reputable group of directors for the hospital and the HMO: John Reeves, Robert Chappell, and Jim Thrower from the business community, Harrold Farrow and Will Holt from the medical community, and police commander Crear Mitchell from law enforcement.

But my task to save the hospital was a virtual impossibility. With the help of this dedicated board of directors and staff, we managed to keep the doors open for only a few weeks. There were no payments coming from Blue Cross, Medicare, Medicaid, or any other commercial insurer. The only source of funds was from LifeChoice HMO operated by the talented and skilled Robin Barclay.

In our attempt to keep the hospital open, we gained permission to use LifeChoice funds and we borrowed from Blue Cross. In spite of all our efforts, we were forced to close the hospital and sell the HMO to satisfy creditors.

This was a new and very challenging experience for me. I was fortunate to have secured the services of an experienced bankruptcy firm, Schafer, Weiner, and Baum. Without their help, it is likely that none of the creditors or employees would have been paid anything. In recognizing our efforts, the U.S. Attorney felt we did the best that could be done under the most difficult circumstances. At least most of the employees and creditors got something, and the HMO was sold to another that maintained the membership and services. Ten years later, I was still wrapping up the affairs of a failed Black institution that fought against the odds and lost. It was a loss to Detroit, the Black community, and Black doctors and hospital administrators who had something to prove.

The Challenge of Golf

I was never very athletic. It was not in my genes, and all of my efforts to alter this genetic deficiency failed miserably. Notwithstanding this lack of natural ability, I was lured into the web of golf. For those who have not tried this test of athleticism, designed by the Devil himself, you will not understand a mixture of pleasure and agony that can coexist simultaneously within the same person. That is my definition of golf.

In spite of a very busy medical practice, I did find time for fun. I thoroughly enjoyed hunting for birds, both quail and dove in season, which carried me through the falls and early winters. When the spring would come, I sought out other recreational activities. Golf caught my attention.

My exposure to golf at that time was limited to only pictures of golfers and beautiful golf courses. In my hometown of Americus, there was a private, White-only golf club. Blacks could only enter the golf course as caddies. My parents were somewhat protective and did not permit me or my brother to "stoop" to being a servants to affluent White men as caddies, so we never even came close to the golf course.

The fascination with golf did not diminish with time, and my enthusiasm even increased when I discovered Black men in Albany played golf at the local Army air base. One of the golfers, Dick Gay, was the owner of the pool parlor that was beneath my office. Dick took great delight in having me stop in his pool parlor between patient visits to destroy me at the pool table. (You might have guessed —I was not very good at shooting pool, either.) I think that I enjoyed the humiliation as much as the pool sharks enjoyed inflicting it on me. It was a pleasant diversion from work.

When I learned that Dick and his buddies regularly would go to the Army air base to play golf, I began to think that perhaps I could try it. I did not have any of the necessary equipment for golf, yet I began making plans to go.

It was coincidental that a serviceman came to my office on a Saturday afternoon with plans for a heavy date, but he had no money —not unusual for a serviceman near the end of a pay period. He wanted to borrow $40 from me with a promise to pay it back on payday.

I initially declined his request, telling him I would not consider it without some security. He had a complete set of MacGregor golf clubs. I had no idea of their value, so I asked Dick. He said that I could not possibly lose on this loan, and he offered to purchase the clubs should the serviceman fail to return. With that assurance, I made the loan, and the serviceman never did come back. Dick wanted to make good on his offer, but I had a better idea. I would start playing golf. Never did I consider taking lessons or practicing before taking to the golf course. I thought: How hard could it be?

No one could tell me that I could not play this game, for I had noticed how easy it was on television. I only realized how wrong I was when I reached the first tee and called on the caddie to give me a club.

He asked, "What club?"

They aren't all alike? I pointed to the first club that I saw, whereupon the caddies all had a good laugh. I had pointed to a 5-iron to hit a shot on a straightaway par-5 golf hole. For those who don't play, it

The Challenge of Golf

was a rookie mistake. I learned many lessons on that first day on a golf course, starting with don't go to a golf course until and unless you take some lessons and visit a practice range.

My golf career, if you can call it that, was interrupted by the Albany Movement and did not resume until many years later when I was a senior resident in Detroit. This is not to say that my golf game ever improved very much, but as I took some lessons and practiced, I began to understand that there is a difference in the golf clubs, and I enjoyed it more.

When I resumed my golfing foray, I sought golfers who were either at my playing skill level or golfers who were willing to tolerate me. It is a good thing that I never took my golfing seriously, for I would have been a basket case after a wayward tee shot or a missed three-foot putt. I could not always tell whether or not my golfing companions were laughing at me, or with me. The one consolation I had was that some with whom I played were at least as bad, if not worse.

I always looked forward to the golf trips that we took together. There were Floyd and Bobbett Meachum, Earl and Sandra Gray, Bob and Robbie Young, Rudy and Doris Poe, Clarence and Valerie Hudson and Bob and Myrna Langford. We all were lousy golfers, but no one could have had more fun. Whether at Palmer Park, Fox Lake, Boyne Country, or any other of the many golf courses that we frequented, we always left the golf course record intact, even when our less-than-skilled performance had seriously damaged the condition of the course.

My golf story would not be complete without including the many years of playing with a large heterogeneous group made up of dentists, accountants, lawyers, physicians, and businessmen. We had all levels of golf ability, and we were grouped accordingly.

Big Jim, "Wishful," Ben G, Cooper, Hutch, Hal, Ted, and others with aliases made up the regular Saturday morning golfing group. The betting was heavy, sometimes as much as a $2 Nassau (a Nassau is a type of wager in golf, and this was anything but a large bet). It was a fun group that endured for many years. We did not set any records in golf, with the possible exception of wearing out our welcome at most of the area golf courses. Yes, it was a loud, fun, and sometimes rowdy group.

As water seeks its own level with the gravitational pull of the earth, I found my level of golf with two osteopathic physicians at the far ends of the United States. I found great joy and satisfaction in challenging my good friends, Don Krpan from California and Phil Shettle from Florida. Don, Phil, and I never passed up the opportunity to play a round of golf, especially when they were active in the AOA at the board level.

The fierce competition that existed between Don and me became legendary in the profession. There were wagers placed on the outcome, sometimes reaching as much as a $5 Nassau. Over many decades, the same dollars changed hands but rarely any "new" money was put in the game. On the rare occasion when Don won, he made certain that everyone knew. He would wait until there was an audience, even with 100 people present, to announce his winnings and he insisted on me making a public statement about how he won.

Don learned how to distract me while playing golf. He often gave me a choice of listening to him sing or indulging in one of his other detrimental passions. They both give me a headache, so it is a difficult choice to make. We were such great friends that we agreed to keep playing as long as we could make it to the golf course.

We coerced Phil into joining our competition, primarily so I had someone that I could beat on occasion. Phil proved to be a big disappointment to me because his game steadily improved once he discovered "Natural Golf." I found it necessary to recruit other golfers with talents that were nearer to mine. That was hard to find.

I should mention that Don was a liberal Democrat and Phil a conservative Republican. One may ask, "How can such ideological opposites be so compatible at golf and be such good friends?" When I find the answer, I will write another book, but I guess it means that

The Challenge of Golf

friendships can transcend even political differences when there is a common interest.

My passion for golf did not diminish with time—it increased, as I found more time to play. My interest naturally led to a desire to join a club. Norma and I would frequently drive by Plum Hollow Golf Club, and I would say, "One day I am going to join." We would have a hearty laugh, for we knew that there was an unwritten policy that Blacks were not accepted into the membership.

Even when we lived on Fairway Drive, right on the Detroit Club course, Blacks were still precluded from becoming members. It was painful to me, as I could stand in my backyard, gazing at the beautifully manicured fairway, and yet could not join the club.

I was so frustrated at living on a golf course I could not join that I threatened to put a picket line around the course. I was restrained by one of my more level-headed neighbors who admonished me, "You throw up a picket line, force them out, and this becomes a low-income, subsidized, slum house project, then what happens to your property value?" This caused me to reassess my strategy for gaining membership.

I temporarily settled for chipping and putting on the sixth hole of the course that bordered my home. This was not exactly an acceptable arrangement for the club members, but there was little that they could do about it. Even the club security guards could not keep me away from the 40-foot easement that separated my property from the golf club. They would have had to hire a special guard for me and my neighbor, Jessie Tolbert, a surgeon and friend who also lived on the golf course and played the sixth hole with me regularly.

This pattern of exclusion of Blacks continued until pressure began to mount from elected officials who belonged to the club. It was difficult for them to solicit the necessary votes from Black members of the legislature and, at the same time, belong to segregated country clubs.

The final straw that broke the back of segregation in country clubs came from the most unlikely place: Birmingham, Alabama. It was at Shoal Creek Country Club where the Professional Golfers Association of America refused to bring a golf tournament as long as their exclusion policy was in place. Again, money and prestige, along with a little political pressure, prevailed. Many private clubs across the country began to open their doors to Blacks and other minorities.

Wabeek Country Club, Pine Knob, and Indian Woods were the exceptions. These private clubs accepted Blacks as members long before it was popular. Although many miles from my home, I joined Wabeek. The club was fully integrated from the time it was built: a beautiful golf course with rolling hills, valleys, and plenty of water. Whenever I needed to punish myself, I would visit Wabeek, originally designed by Jack Nicklaus, who I believe had a disdain for weekend golfers. I tortured myself for several years at Wabeek until other opportunities for club membership became available.

Some years later, I decided to join a club closer to home, Western Golf and Country Club. I knew many members who were professional colleagues, and we were on friendly terms. In spite of this, no one offered to sponsor me for membership. Perhaps they never considered that I would want to join a private golf club. This was reminiscent of "The Invisible Man." I did not exist as a golf club member in their minds.

Finally, one of the Western members did say, "I would like to sponsor you, but they would promptly ask for my membership." He said that it was unlikely I would be accepted. It never occurred to him that perhaps he should not belong to a club that would not accept his "friend" without regard to their race or religion.

I eventually found a sponsor at Western and applied along with another Black, Ben Grier, a lawyer and friend. I was accepted, but Ben was denied membership, with no reason given except to say, "We have our quota."

I was not quite sure which quota they were referencing, but I soon concluded, "Black quota." I asked the membership committee and board of directors to reconsider their rejection of Ben's application and in the event that the "quota" was total membership, assure Ben of

The Challenge of Golf

the next vacancy. They refused, so I promptly rescinded my acceptance.

I was determined that I would not be the "only one," nor would I be the token, nor "the spook that sat by the door," nor the person "who forgot his friend at the door." Over the fierce apologetic objection of many of my member "friends," I stood firm, as did the governing board of Western. My application fee was in part refunded, and I turned my attention to another club that I had dreamed about for many years.

Plum Hollow had just begun to accept Blacks as members, with Ray Jenson and Herman Glass the first to be accepted. Ted White and I decided to apply. Together, we were interviewed by the chairman of the membership committee. The chairman was not very encouraging because they already had two. We were certain he was thinking, *There goes the country club.*

Ted and I looked at each other when the chairman asked if we would be embarrassed if the committee turned us down for membership. "Us? Embarrassed? We've been turned down all of our lives, so rejection is no stranger to us."

The chairman was convinced that we met all the other qualifications for membership, so there was no legitimate reason for denying us. He braced himself and said, "If you are willing to take the risk of embarrassment, then I am willing to recommend you for membership."

We were accepted, and to the credit of the chairman, he was the first to invite us to lunch as members. He reported, "I have not heard one word of complaint about your acceptance into Plum Hollow." We played golf with him often, and other members began to accept us and invite us to play.

"It's not me, it's them" was never more evident than at Plum Hollow Golf Club. Many Whites who wanted to be friendly and closer to Blacks whom they enjoyed, feared for what their other friends and neighbors would think, say, or do. Thankfully, great strides have been made in the past 30 years.

My Religion

I could never consider myself a religious fanatic, but I have always been an active church member. I am Baptist by chance and not necessarily by choice. I was not given the opportunity to make a choice because of my father, who was a devoted, dyed-in-the-wool Baptist. During my childhood I spent many, many hours in church. My father held every possible office that any one person could hold in a church. In addition to being a deacon and trustee, he was superintendent of the Sunday school, and director of the choir, in which he also sang and played the piano. When there was money to count, he acted as treasurer.

My father and mother were dedicated to Bethesda Baptist Church in Americus, and they made certain that their children were taught to respect religion. We joined the church at an early age, and throughout our lives, we have continued to attend and participate.

My oldest son once asked, "Dad, why do you still go to church regularly and participate in so many church activities?"

My response was simple: "I have never known life outside of the church, and I have had a good life. Whether my good fortune is because of the church has not been a consideration. I do not know what life would be like had the church not been a part of it, and frankly, do not want to chance that other life."

The church has played an important role in developing my confidence in interaction with other people. It was in the church that I discovered that I could comfortably speak to large groups. As important, I thoroughly enjoy many of the church services, especially good music from the anthems to the spirituals to the gospel songs. I also enjoy a good-spirited preacher in the tradition of the Southern Black Baptist. There is nothing more thrilling in my life than to hear a good, dynamic, and informative sermon.

I have been privileged to hear some of the greatest preachers of my day, including Martin Luther King Jr., who was one of the greatest orators of all time, as well as William Holmes Borders, Sandy Ray, J. Raymond Henderson, Cornell Talley, and Vernon Johns.

I have heard sermons by Charles Gilchrist Adams, Wyatt Tee Walker, Freddie Haynes, Joseph Roberts, and the unconquerable Jeremiah H. Wright Jr. These are some of the best that our nation has ever produced. Not only are they spiritually stimulating but intellectually challenging and culturally motivating.

I cannot say that my motivation for staying in the church is solely to nourish my soul, which is important to me, but I also stay because I am very comfortable there. I experience a peace that can rarely be found elsewhere. I am fortunate that my wife and I could often share that calm. She was always more religious than me, yet we found common ground in our faith.

After Norma and I married and moved to Atlanta, we joined her family church, Wheat Street Baptist. The pastor was William Holmes Borders, who was recognized as "the radio preacher." His best-selling book, *Seven Minutes on the Mike*, was revolutionary for Black preachers in the early 1950s.

My interest in the church continued when I entered Des Moines Still College of Osteopathy in Iowa. My studies and my work did not keep me from becoming an active member of Corinthian Baptist Church. I even taught Sunday school and sang in the male chorus.

My Religion

We called ourselves "The Song Fellows," and we sang whenever we had the opportunity. We were technically not very good, but we enjoyed every minute of our singing.

I continued my church activities during my internship, but the rigorous schedule and pressures of internship limited my involvement.

In Albany, where I elected to practice, I again became a very active church member at the historic Mt. Zion Baptist Church. The pastor, E. James Grant, became a key figure in the Albany Movement. In addition, the Rev. Grant was principal of a school in Baker County, notorious for being one of the most racist schools in the South. If there was any group that the citizens of Baker County hated more than Blacks, it was the "carpet-bagging, nigger-loving northern Whites." Most travelers, including commercial truckers, avoided Baker County like the plague.

Occasionally, I would have to travel through Baker County to see a patient or to get to the only hospital that I could use in Bainbridge, Georgia. As committed as I was to nonviolence, I still carried a loaded pistol on the front seat of my car when traveling through Baker. I was determined that should a Baker County policeman stop me, I would accept the ticket, but I would not go to jail. Several Blacks arrested there were never to be seen again. We had every reason to believe they were lynched, which was not an uncommon occurrence in Georgia prior to the Civil Rights Era. I did not want to become a statistic among the missing.

Reverend Grant, after the loss of his position as principal and under the constant threat of harm, still opened his church to the Albany Movement for its many mass rallies. I shall always admire him for his undaunting courage and commitment to the cause of justice. It was the courage of Revs. Grant, Boyd, Gay, Wells, Smith, and other preachers and pastors who gave their unqualified support to the movement that sustained me. I can say without equivocation or fear of contradiction, that were it not for the churches and their pastors and preachers, the Civil Rights Movement could not have possibly succeeded. Here was a relevance found in the church that I had not anticipated in my youth, with even greater meaning and significance—spiritually, socially, civically, and politically.

When we were preparing to leave Albany, Martin Luther King Jr. recommended two churches. The first was the Second Baptist Church in Greek Town, the site of one of the stops on the Underground Railroad that holds great significance in the flight of slaves from the South en route to Canada. The second recommendation was New Light Baptist Church, an established church that was built by the legendary Rev. A. M. Martin.

Reverend Talley, pastor at New Light, was well-known as one of the best Gospel preachers in Detroit. Talley was a spell-binding preacher who could tell a Bible story better than anyone that we had ever heard. New Light also had outstanding choirs and an organist who enlivened the church service. We felt at home there.

We stayed with Rev. Talley and New Light Church for many years and became close friends. Reverend Tally, his wife Martha, and their three children were all like family. I took care of their medical needs, and Rev. Talley took care of our spiritual needs. It was not at all unusual for Rev. Talley to visit our home in the wee hours of the night or early morning just to talk.

It was with great sadness that we found it necessary to leave New Light. Martin Luther King Jr. had publicly criticized the United States' involvement in Vietnam, considering it an unjust war. For this, Martin was severely criticized by many who had supported him from the beginning of the Montgomery bus boycott. Our pastor, Rev. Talley, joined the chorus of those who not only criticized Martin but also withdrew support from the Southern Christian Leadership Conference, Martin's organization. Because of what Martin Luther King Jr. and the Southern Christian Leadership Conference meant to us personally and as a race of people, we could not in good conscience stay in New Light. Martin and the cause to which he devoted his life were more important to us than any single church.

We later joined New Prospect Baptist Church, which was close to

My Religion

home, and we fell in love with the pastor, his family, and the many people who filled his congregation. The Rev. Sam Leon Whitney became a close friend, and we grew as close to the Whitneys as we had been to the Talleys. I took great pride in caring for the Whitney family, and we stayed with New Prospect for many years until we relocated to Southfield, a suburb of Detroit.

We then joined Hartford Memorial Baptist Church, where we would stay for more than 20 years. Reverend Charles Gilchrist Adams was dynamic, and his thought-provoking sermons kept us coming back for more. We again grew very close to our pastor and his family. The Rev. Adams and I share a middle name, Gilchrist, and we kept promising to research our family tree to discover the link.

The Rev. Adams had boundless energy, and one of my constant objectives was to get him to slow down. But that proved improbable as he was born to be what he was: a great preacher and leader. In addition to his pastoral duties, he served as president of the Detroit branch of the NAACP and president of the Progressive National Baptist Convention. I shall always remember him with great fondness. His invocation at my inauguration as president of the American Osteopathic Association was one of the most memorable in the history of the organization.

He was also one of the first presenters for the award-winning Michigan State University College of Osteopathic Medicine Visiting Minority Faculty Series, "*From Slavery to Freedom: An American Odyssey.*" He was also present when I received the coveted Honorary Doctor of Science degree from Michigan State University. Thus, it should be no surprise that Rev. Adams was also chosen to perform the marriage ceremony for my youngest daughter, Dee-Dee.

Church will continue to be an important part of my life, for without it, there would be a void that could never be filled by any other institution, organization, or activity.

All Our Children

Norma and I were quite fortunate to have five terrific children. All are fiercely independent, sometimes to a fault. That is a trait that was instilled in them, of which we were proud. Each has a different and unique personality that made for a very interesting and challenging family life.

We considered it a success in raising children in that none were on drugs, in jail, or having children out of wedlock. All are ambitious, innovative, and have a thirst for knowledge. Thus, they all finished college and continued in graduate school and some into the learned professions.

Laurita

Our firstborn, Laurita, is the closest thing to a "Benjamin Spock" baby as we had. Her earliest days were spent in the home of Norma's mother, Mary Smith. Laurita, called "Rita," was probably the most pampered of our five children. It was not unusual for Mother Mary and Rita to be sitting up in bed reading, singing, or sipping a beverage late into the night or in the wee hours of the morning.

William G Anderson, DO, FACOS

Rita gave Mother Mary the nickname of "Dear," and it stuck forever thereafter. Dear was one of the most remarkable women that I have ever known. As a single, divorced mother of four, she managed to provide for all of their needs and encouraged and supported them through college.

The first few years of our marriage were spent with Mother Mary, and she took me in as one of her own. She defied all the stereotypes of the nagging mother-in-law. One could not have had a more loving, caring mother-in-law.

Rita, in her quest for independence in thought and action, was on occasion defiant and reluctant to seek or accept advice from us, her parents. This trait was carried into her adult life.

In spite of this trait, or perhaps because of it, Rita graduated from one the oldest and most prestigious Black colleges in the United States, Fisk College in Nashville, Tennessee.

With a Fisk degree in hand, Rita was recruited to enter the job market with the promise of becoming a buyer for Bloomingdale's, a major department store in New York. It was virtually impossible to persuade Rita that New York was one of the most difficult cities in the country in which to live and get started on a career, and that becoming a buyer for a major department store was an unrealistic goal.

That is when her fierce independence and the lure of adventure in worldwide travel as a buyer took over. We were left with no alternative but to support her in this endeavor. It brought tears to our eyes to see the conditions in which she lived in New York, but she pursued her dream and did become a buyer at Bloomingdale's!

Realization set in, and the pressures of living in New York began to wear on Rita, but it was there that she met her husband-to-be, a recent Harvard Law School graduate with a promising career, Willie "Mack" Faison. Mack was a tall, handsome, very intelligent man with a subtle sense of humor. He was offered a position with one of the largest law firms in the Midwest, and to our delight, they moved from the jungles of New York to the more livable city of Detroit.

"Spockism" entered into the marriage and disrupted what we all had hoped to be a lasting, happy relationship. "You do your thing, and I do my thing" and yet be married was the mantra of the Spock generation.

Rita would be challenged by a series of unexpected events that led to divorce, but she was not deterred and continued her pursuit of independence. With their son, Maxwell, she began to build another life for herself in Detroit and grew closer and closer to us, especially her mother. She built a successful career as a Girl Scout regional manager. Then as a project director in the Detroit Empowerment Zone, she handled a $20 million portfolio. She also worked for Traveler's Aid and finished her eclectic career as a librarian after 17 years at the Southfield Public Library. Maxwell, a graduate of Michigan State University, has chosen a career in airport security.

William "Gil" Gilchrist

Our secondborn was given my name, William Gilchrist Anderson II. He is the second William Gilchrist but the third William Anderson. Thus, he is not William Jr.

To distinguish between us, he is called Gil.

Gil was the most determined to show his independence. To demonstrate this fierce drive, he emancipated himself while still in college. He wanted to prove to himself and others that he was well capable of caring for himself.

The strategy of independence worked well for Gil until there were needs that could not be met without the help and support of family. Of course, Norma and I were proud of his ambition to become independent, and we would only provide advice, financial help, or other support when he asked.

Gil graduated from the most prestigious college for Black men in the nation, Morehouse College in Atlanta. Morehouse has probably produced more Black professionals than any other college in the country. My father and brother, both Morehouse Men, no doubt influenced his choice. My father started the indoctrination of my sons at an early age. He told them there was no better college in the world. It was not surprising that both of our sons would choose Morehouse.

Gil made us very proud when he chose a career in osteopathic medicine. I have been asked on many occasions, "How did you get your children to choose careers in osteopathic medicine?" My answer is that neither Norma nor I tried to influence our children to enter the field of medicine. We only insisted that they get a good education that would prepare them for a useful and productive life. This can also be interpreted to mean, "Get an education that gets you out of the house and on your own."

I would like to believe that my children saw in me a love for osteopathic medicine and that it has provided a very comfortable livelihood. They saw the hours and the sacrifices that Norma and I made to get to where we are, but they also saw the rewards. The rewards have far outweighed the sacrifices.

Gil and I were in practice together for the first few years after his graduation from a residency in OB-GYN. He is a very fine, skilled, knowledgeable, and ethical physician. There are few satisfactory experiences that can equal performing delicate and complex surgery with your son and learning from him. Such has been our relationship. He would yet on occasion boost my ego by asking an opinion on a complex medical problem.

He opened an OB-GYN practice a short distance from where we had practiced together. That was a very smart move on his part, and it was deserving of congratulations. .

Ultimately, Gil moved his private practice from Detroit to Livonia, where he served as director of osteopathic education and program director for the osteopathic internship at Saint Mary Mercy Hospital. He is now fully retired.

Gil was smart enough, or lucky enough, to marry a college sweetheart, Doris, who was a student at neighboring Spelman College.

All Our Children

Doris has been a stabilizing force in his life. Together, they have produced a boy and a girl of extraordinary talent.

Shannon, the firstborn, has a personality and a charm that radiates. She was the first graduate of Hampton College from the family. She completed two master's degrees: one in school counseling from Western Michigan University, and a second in special education at Wayne State University. Children come to love her, and she does well as an educator and counselor.

Barrett Gilchrist, the second of the Gil-Doris union, has genius potential. Barrett can excel in anything that he desires to do. As a pianist, he won every trophy available in his music class for several years. At the University of Michigan, he majored in pre-med and Japanese. Yes, I said Japanese. He has studied Japanese since his pre-teens and regularly communicates with his Japanese friends in their language. He expressed a desire to go into osteopathic medicine, and Gil asked him where he would elect to go to medical school. Barrett responded with a series of questions.

"Dad, you are an osteopathic physician, aren't you? Big Daddy (that's me) is an osteopathic physician, isn't he ... so aren't Uncle Frank, Aunt Dee, and Uncle Gary, all osteopathic physicians, too?"

Gil answered yes to all. Then Barrett stated emphatically, "I'm not going to break the family tradition." End of discussion. He attended the Michigan State University College of Osteopathic Medicine.

Barrett and I have a peculiar bond that was discovered when he was but a toddler. We share a love for computers. I started as the teacher but soon became the student. Barrett teaches me much about computer technology. I take great pride in the influence that I had on Barrett by exposing him to the latest, sophisticated computer technology at a very early age.

That early love of osteopathic medicine and computers is now melded in Barrett's outstanding career. He is now a specialist in robotic urologic surgery for the Detroit Medical Center.

Valé Jeanita

Our next child was Valé Jeanita, born while I was a first-year medical student. We came to call her Jenny; others later called her Valé. She was always Jenny to us.

Jenny was a cross between Rita and Gil in that she would listen to advice from us and selectively choose to follow that which best fit her plans. She was a bright student who, without hesitation, chose to attend Spelman College in Atlanta, the most prestigious college for Black women in the nation.

Jenny's first manifestation of independence became evident when she chose to remain in Atlanta after graduation from Spelman. This said to us, her mother and father, "I am ready to branch out on my own and really don't need the security of home anymore." This is not to suggest that the distance between us lessened the bond. She remains in almost daily contact.

She continued her education in graduate school, got married to Stanley Henson, had three beautiful children, and stayed in Atlanta. She chose a career in social work, where she had the most interest. Her career has been remarkable, as she has worked herself through the ranks and bureaucracies of government in the Department of Social Services and the juvenile judicial system. Now retired, her work with children and youth in foster care and adoption was widely acclaimed throughout the state of Georgia.

Jenny's daughters all excelled in their pursuits. Erika, the eldest and the "late bloomer," searched for several years before she found a career that would both interest and challenge her. She found law.

After experiencing life in the real world, independent of the comforts of home, Erika came to the conclusion that there was more to what she was doing. We are very proud that when she found herself, she, on her own volition, returned to her education and received a journalism degree from Loyola University New Orleans, then a J.D. from Vermont Law School.

Erika was aware of a standing rule in the Anderson family: "You stay in school or get a job." To stay in school meant continuing support, financial and whatever else was needed.

Erika now marries her passion for environmental conservation, historic preservation, and the law working as a historian and site protector for the Georgia Department of Transportation in Atlanta. She is the author of the book *The Food Holiday: Uganda*. She has a daughter, Iman, who is attending Kennesaw State University.

Camille, the second of Jenny's daughters, takes great pride in how she looks and acts. I often refer to her as "Madame Queen." Camille made us all proud when she chose to go to Hampton College, the second in the Anderson family to attend that exceptional Black institution.

Camille too chose a career in osteopathic medicine, graduating from Edward Via College of Osteopathic Medicine at Virginia Tech University. She then earned a Ph.D. in health promotion and international medicine at Virginia Tech, traveling to the Dominican Republic to do her research. She completed her residency at Sinai-Grace Hospital in Detroit, and now practices internal medicine in Tallahassee, Florida.

Her husband, Fitz Blake, is an emergency medicine physician at Tallahassee Memorial Hospital, and they have three children: Sydney, Clinton, and Emery.

The third and last of the Anderson-Henson girls is Fatima, another star student. Fatima has a winning personality and achieved exceptional grades in all her classes. Fatima was likely to succeed in any career that she chose; her decision was the law and education. She is an alumna of American University and the University of Miami. She taught high school history and government for years. Admitted to the bar in Georgia, Washington D.C., and Florida, she is an education attorney. Fatima is also the author of the award-winning young adult novel *Love in the Age of Dragons* and the children's book *Courageous Cody's Western Adventure*.

Frank Lewis

The fourth of our children is Frank Lewis. Frank was the most mischievous and adventurous of our children. As a very young child, he was unpredictable and could always find a way to get into trouble —nothing malicious, but frequently aggravating and tormenting his parents.

On occasion, Norma and I would go on vacation without the children. We would instruct the babysitter to yell out every few minutes, "Stop, Frank!" as it was almost certain that Frank would be up to another of his mischievous acts.

Frank survived his childhood. More appropriately, we, his parents, survived his childhood. He too is one of the "late bloomers" in the Anderson family. Perhaps this is a yet undiscovered genetic trait.

Notwithstanding the late "bloom," Frank was searching for his place in society, and attended both Morehouse College and the University of Michigan, receiving a degree in general studies. It took Frank time to figure out what he wanted to do next, as he could choose anything, and later we found out. He would choose osteopathic medicine.

After a false start in medical school, his marriage, and the birth of his daughter, Brittany, Frank worked as a microbiologist, financial analyst, and pharmaceutical representative. This he did for a few years until his ambition kicked in, and he decided that he really wanted to pursue being an osteopathic physician. It is not unusual to find pharmaceutical representatives who are very smart and very capable in what they do. Many of us in the practice of medicine have come to depend on these reps for current information on drugs and their use. Many of these reps later become physicians. Thus was the case with Frank.

That "independent" gene took control over the life of Frank, and he made an unexpected move in the manner and style of his cousin, Erika. Frank, on his own initiative, returned to osteopathic medical school and graduated from the University of Health Sciences in Kansas City, Missouri.

Following graduation, Frank fell under the influence of his brother Gil rather than me and decided on a career as an obstetrician and gynecologist. Licensed in five states, Frank works as a traveling OB-GYN hospitalist. His daughter, Brittany, works as a registered nurse in Myrtle Beach. His grandchildren include Zavier, Charlie, and Penelope.

Frank has had a distinguished career as an obstetrician, and he is a talented and gifted surgeon. I cannot say that the surgical talents of my sons come from me, but should you draw that conclusion, I will not challenge it.

Darnita Dawn

Norma and I must have learned how to raise children from our previous four experiences. Our fifth and last child was as near perfect as one could be. She did everything that the ideal child should do. Never was Darnita Dawn a problem child. We all call her Dee-Dee and she, from birth, has continued until today to be *my baby*.

Dee-Dee followed in the footsteps of her older sister, Jenny, and entered Spelman College. After graduating from Spelman, she announced her choice of career. To no one's surprise, she chose to become an osteopathic physician.

Dee-Dee graduated from Michigan State University College of Osteopathic Medicine and interned at Detroit Osteopathic Hospital.

It was at DOH that Dee-Dee met her husband-to-be, Gary Hill. Gary was a graduate of the Philadelphia College of Osteopathic Medicine and a resident in internal medicine.

Gary finished his residency and moved to Gadsden, Alabama, where he was assigned to fulfill a public health commitment. Dee-Dee followed her heart, now firmly attached to Gary, and elected to serve a residency in Chattanooga, Tennessee. The long-distance relationship did not meet either of their expectations. To get closer together, Dee-Dee moved to Birmingham, where she completed her residency at Carraway Methodist Hospital.

Dee-Dee and Gary practiced in the same health system in Gadsden for several years after Gary completed his public health obligation. The practice conditions were near ideal, but the town of Gadsden left much to be desired. They relocated to southern Florida, where Gary joined the faculty of Nova Southeastern University College of Osteopathic Medicine and Dee-Dee joined the staff of Jackson Memorial Hospital. Dee-Dee maintains family medicine practices at various health centers throughout the state of Alabama. She is also the author of the book *Blacks in Osteopathic Medicine: An Idea Whose Time Has Come*. Gary serves as associate dean of clinical education and officer for diversity, equity, and inclusion at Edward Via College of Osteopathic Medicine.

Dee-Dee and Gary have added to our bevy of grandchildren. Aliyah and Amirah, their first two, have stolen our hearts. I bonded with Aliyah when she was only six weeks old. She and I together attended an AOA convention and spent many hours getting to know each other. To the amazement of many, Aliyah was carried around the convention activities on my hip without so much as a whimper. She became attached to me and me to her. A week does not pass without us at least talking on the phone. She keeps me abreast of everything that is going on in the Anderson-Hill family, even some things that her parents do not wish to be told. Such are children and grandchildren.

Amirah came a year later, and we immediately became attached as with Aliyah. The two girls are a joy to be with. Likewise, a week does not pass when we do not see each other or talk on the phone. The two are very bright and at an early age, could already converse in Spanish and French. They attended a French school and studied Spanish, the latter almost a necessity in southern Florida.

The girls and I have a secret between us that is not shared with anyone. We never end a conversation without the disclosure of the secret. This is probably the only secret that they keep from everybody, including their parents.

The last of the Anderson-Hill children and our grandchildren is Mika'l. That is a name that you try to pronounce, but do not try to spell. As children, Aliyah and Amirah gave Mika'l all of the attention that he wanted and more.

Now grown, Aliyah is a graduate of Tuskegee University who pursued occupational therapy. Amirah is an osteopathic family physician in Columbus, Georgia, and Mika'l pursued engineering at Auburn University.

Norma and I could be no prouder of our children, grandchildren, and great-grandchildren. I attribute what they have become to the sometimes-tough love of Norma. She was the stabilizing force in all of our lives. All our children looked to Mother and Grandmother for comfort, counsel, and advice. She gave it liberally and lovingly.

Norma and I had always been close to our children, and to some, closer than others, apparently depending on the gender. Not unlike other families, Norma was closer to the males, and I was closer to the female members of the family. A phenomenon that I don't fully understand, nor do I try to understand it. I just accept it.

It took a near tragedy in our family for us to realize how close we are psychologically and emotionally as well as physically. For me, that near tragedy occurred when our Dee-Dee was scheduled for a surgical procedure. What began as a routine surgery almost developed into a major, complex, and complicated procedure. Because of the nature of the procedure and the desire to have her in the hands of the best-qualified surgeon, her husband and the rest of the family urged her to come to Detroit.

The day of the surgery was fraught with anxiety and anticipation, as the minor procedure began to develop into a major one. The apprehension turned to near panic when the surgeon reported early in the surgery that he had discovered some unanticipated pathology that caused concern. He made several visits to us in the surgical waiting room to make progress reports on Dee-Dee's condition. It did not help that the pathologist suggested that a rare cancer may be involved, and further study was necessary to confirm the diagnosis.

I have never felt closer to one of our children as I did on that day. It was most difficult to fight back the feeling of impending doom as the potential of losing a child, my child, dominated my mind. She was in surgery for what seemed to be an eternity. I never left the hospital during the entire ordeal, and of course, I found it almost impossible to relax, let alone rest. During surgery, I believe that I felt every stroke of the surgeon's knife, and I only breathed as Dee-Dee breathed. Norma was the calmest, as was typical of her in stressful situations. Gary was near tears. Gil was constantly going in and out of the operating room bringing back messages on the progress of the surgery. All of the family was in anxious anticipation of the outcome.

The surgery went well, as Dee-Dee was in excellent health. I am certain that she tolerated it better than the rest of the family, especially me. After an extended time in recovery, Dee-Dee was carried to her room. I asked and was given permission to spend the night in the hospital room. A cot was provided, and I never left her side until she was fully recovered from the anesthetic and was sitting up and talking.

I have never felt more relief than when the pathology report was returned, and it was *benign*!

It took this near tragedy for me to come to the realization of just how close a parent can be to their child. Our bodies, mind, and spirit were as one.

A Brush with Death

I always felt as though I were immortal. After all, I have enjoyed excellent health, and I have remained physically active. Although I was never very good at any particular athletic activity, I did play some football, baseball, and basketball. Though I had a limit to my physical activity, it was never seriously tested, even during basic training in the Navy. I always felt as though there was a remaining, untapped, reserve power that was just waiting to be called on. That attitude remained until the real test came. My mind would tell me that I could continue to do the same things that I had done earlier in life as my body aged. I discovered that my body was aging faster than my mind. My mind would say, "You can do it," but my body would say, "No you can't."

It was in the fall of a year that, chronologically, I was well into my eighth decade of life. We had developed a leak in our roof following a season of heavy rain. My mind said, "You can get up on that 12-foot ladder and repair that leaky roof."

You can better understand this potential conflict between my mind and my body when you learn that I have never been a carpenter or roofer, so my experience with 12-foot ladders and roof repairs was severely limited. But, with the prospect of saving hundreds of dollars and gaining the satisfaction of performing a task that challenged me, I yielded to my mind in spite of the message that my body was sending.

I succeeded in reaching the top of the ladder without any assistance or critical observers. However, my repair job on the roof was permanently interrupted when, without any advance warning, the ladder came crashing down with a loud thud. The crash was the ladder, and the thud was my head striking the concrete below.

My wife, who was in the kitchen near the site of this misadventure, heard the loud clatter and came running, only to find me sprawled out on the concrete garage floor with the ladder lying across me. She removed the ladder from my crumpled body and attempted to help me up, as it was obvious that I had just had an unplanned, premature, and rapid descent from the ladder.

As she reached down to help me up, I resisted, stating, "Just let me lie here for a while so that I can contemplate the stupid thing that I have just done."

I did not know where to feel first. There was pain in my head, back, legs, and arms. It was difficult to determine where I hurt the most. In retrospect, I think I hurt most in my pride, the kind of "pride hurt" that goes along with failure in the performance of what was to be a simple task for which I was ill-prepared.

After a short eternity, lying wounded on the bare concrete, I managed to sit up with the welcomed assistance of my wife. Needless to say, the roof did not get repaired that day or at any future day, by me. My roof-repairing career suddenly and abruptly ended. Besides, my wife promptly called our friend and all-around superior repairman, Herod Jones, and said to him, "Come and get this ladder and never, ever again let my husband come near it. And while you are at it, remove all other ladders over three feet tall."

A little 12-foot fall onto concrete could not deter me from fulfilling my professional and social commitments, even though my body was racked with pain from head to toe. I was not certain which part of my

A Brush with Death

body was hurting the most. It soon became evident that some parts of my body began to feel better, but my head continued to hurt and it became progressively more and more severe.

My first post-fall commitment was to pre-med students at Ohio State University. I never wanted to disappoint students, and this commitment had been made many months earlier. I took a couple of Tylenol and went to bed, hoping that my headache and body pains would be short-lived. I did not feel much better the next morning, but I was determined to go to Columbus. I took more Tylenol and made my way to the airport with a now-throbbing headache. I was met at the airport in Columbus, and I was taken to the campus of Ohio State University, where I spent a more or less miserable few hours, nursing a pounding headache and a wide variety of assorted aches and pains in my back, legs, and arms.

I managed to survive the day in Columbus, and I was looking forward to the comforts of my bed back home the next morning. Much to my dismay, upon reaching the Columbus airport, I discovered that my flight had been canceled. I took more Tylenol and hoped that my headache would soon ease. It didn't. Now I was faced with another dilemma: how to get back home with my increasingly severe headache. I did not relish the thought of renting a car and driving, and I certainly did not want to spend the day at the airport. It was at this moment that fate smiled on me, and I was greeted by a friend and fraternity brother, Bill Pickard. Bill had been in Columbus on business and was also trying to get back to Detroit. He offered me a ride home.

I accepted, and together, we rented a car, and we were on our way back to Detroit. Bill was kind enough to drive the entire distance, much to my relief, as I was in no condition to drive anywhere. The trip back was uneventful, and Bill dropped me off at the airport, where I got my car and drove home, anxious to take more Tylenol and go to bed.

My next commitment was to attend the AOA Convention in San Francisco. This was a weeklong meeting of the Board of Trustees and the annual educational program. I again loaded up on Tylenol and, with Norma, proceeded to the airport for the long trip to San Francisco— longer because of my constant, throbbing headache.

My next commitment was to play golf with Don Krpan at AOA's annual Auxiliary Golf Outing. Playing golf with Don is much akin to having a root canal done without anesthesia, but he was a great friend, and it kept my mind off the headache for a few hours. I survived the golf game and a week of convention activities. The headache continued, now to the point of making my eyes cross. The pain was becoming unbearable, and the Tylenol no longer provided relief. I could hardly wait to get home and to visit my doctor.

Dr. Debra Jo Levan had been my personal physician for several years, and I had the utmost confidence in her. I was in so much pain that I was ready to do anything she told me.

With a smirk, she said, "That's different. You have been coming to me for years, and you've never done anything I have told you before." After a preliminary examination, she referred me to a neurologist.

Dr. Mary Ann Guidice was probably the most thorough neurologist that I had ever met. She immediately ordered a CAT scan and called in a neurosurgeon for consultation. The diagnosis was obvious even to one inexperienced in reading these shadows. I had not one, but two, subdural hematomas, bleeding under the covering of the brain, that were pressing on the brain tissue and producing severe headaches.

Dr. Ricky Olson, an experienced and skilled neurosurgeon, arranged for an early operation to evacuate the hematomas. It was an operation that I describe as "letting the evil spirits out," and I got immediate relief. My stay in the hospital was of a short duration. I was ready to go home the next day and go back to work. My doctors and my wife had other ideas, so I was confined to my home and forbidden to drive for an additional two weeks.

During my house confinement, I relaxed my regular daily grooming. I grew a beard, something that I had always wanted but never had a good reason to try it. Now was that chance, and I had a reason.

A Brush with Death

For those who have not yet tried to grow a beard, be advised: In the beginning, it itches something terrible, especially on the sides and on the neck. The chin growth is much better tolerated.

Before returning to work, I decided to shave off the beard. I started with the side of my face and the neck to get rid of the most annoying areas. Midway through the shave, I was struck by an unexpected new appearance. The sides were gone, and the neck was almost clean-shaven when, all of a sudden, a picture flashed in my mind.

On the cover of the current issue of *Modern Maturity* was a picture of none other than 007 himself, Sir Sean Connery.

I said, "Damn, he looks like me!" The resemblance was remarkable, I thought. The Van Dyke beard looked good on him, so why not leave it on me? After all, I needed a reminder of my brush with death, doing something that I can only call "stupid." Each morning when I looked in the mirror, the beard would remind me not to repeat that disastrous feat and not to do anything stupid today. Some people need to wear a sign that says, *"I am stupid."* It would save a lot of time by early identification. For me, my sign was the Van Dyke beard. I am certain that I will find something else stupid to do, but never again do I plan on climbing a ladder to repair a roof.

I will instead focus my attention on what I do best: spreading the word, inspiring the next generation of community leaders, pursuing inclusion, defending civil rights, and encouraging all I meet to work hard, stay focused, be kind, help others, and follow their dreams.

And thus, the next chapter of bringing people together began.

From Slavery to Freedom: An American Odyssey
Michigan State University's William G. Anderson Esteemed Lecture Series Speakers

During my work as a civil rights activist and an osteopathic physician, I was afforded an opportunity to build strong relationships with founding icons of the American Civil Rights Movement. When I started this lecture series at Michigan State University, I was literally calling on friends, and friends of friends, to share their knowledge and experience. As the series gained national attention, it was simulcast and then archived on YouTube.

Below is a list of speakers, many of whom spoke multiple times throughout the years. This is a "non-duplicative" list but please keep in mind, some of these esteemed speakers spoke three or four times throughout the years, sharing wisdom with the next generation of leaders in America.

William G Anderson, DO, FACOS

2001

- **The Rev. Dr. Charles G. Adams,** first Nickerson Professor, Ethics and Ministry at Harvard Divinity School; senior pastor at Hartford Memorial Baptist Church. Named among 100 most influential Black Americans by *Ebony*.
- **The Rev. Dr. Joseph Lowery,** United Methodist pastor; founder of the Southern Christian Leadership Conference (SCLC); aka "the dean of the Civil Rights Movement." Received the Presidential Medal of Freedom from Barack Obama.
- **The Rev. Dr. Otis Moss, Jr.,** pastor, theologian, speaker, author, and activist. Regional director for the SCLC, participated in Selma march, close confidant of Dr. King. Senior pastor at Olivet Institutional Baptist Church. Adviser to President Jimmy Carter.
- **The Rev. Dr. Wyatt T. Walker,** pastor, theologian, and cultural historian, chief of staff for Martin Luther King. Helped to found CORE (Congress of Racial Equality); executive director of the SCLC. Senior pastor at Canaan Baptist Church of Christ.

2002

- **Dr. Dorothy Cotton,** civil rights activist and educational director for the SCLC. Created the Citizen Education Program and organized the Birmingham Campaign and Children's Crusade.
- **Dick Gregory,** comedian, actor, activist, writer, and social critic. Poking fun at bigotry and racism, he was a staple in comedy clubs, TV, and on records.
- **The Rev. Dr. Jeremiah A. Wright, Jr.,** pastor emeritus of

the Trinity United Church of Christ; the Obama family were members. Activist and author of several books.

2003

- **Tom Hayden,** social and political activist, author, politician, Freedom Rider. A leader in SCLC; one of the "Chicago Seven" who led protests at the 1968 Democratic National Convention. Won seats in the California State Assembly and California State Senate.
- **Dr. Bernice Johnson Reagon,** founder of singing group Sweet Honey in the Rock. Professor of American history at American University, composer, musician, scholar, curator at the Smithsonian, author of several books, and social activist.

2004

- **Juanita Jones Abernathy**, civil rights activist, teacher, and wife of Ralph David Abernathy. Morehouse School of Religion Trustee and director for Metropolitan Atlanta Rapid Transit Authority. Helped organize the Montgomery bus boycott and marched from Selma to Montgomery.
- **The Rev. Dr. Lawrence Edward Carter, Sr.**, first dean of the Martin Luther King International Chapel at Morehouse College; historian, professor, author, curator, and civil rights expert. More than 1,000 speaking engagements, traveled to 38 countries, and broadcast more than 100 times.
- **Dr. Aldon Morris,** emeritus professor of sociology, Northwestern University. Studied social movements, civil rights and social inequality; best known for his work on

W.E.B. Du Bois. Past president of the American Sociological Association.
- **The Rev. Dr. Gardner Calvin Taylor,** grandson of emancipated slaves, became pastor of Concord Baptist Church. Prominent religious leader of the Civil Rights Movement. Awarded Medal of Freedom by President Bill Clinton.

2005

- **Lerone Bennett Jr.,** scholar, author, social historian. Worked as executive director of *Ebony*. First author to publish the relationship between Thomas Jefferson and Sally Hemings.
- **The Rev. Dr. Frederick D. Haynes III,** senior pastor at Friendship-West Baptist Church. Devoted to economic justice and empowerment, transforming the lives of the disenfranchised.
- **The Rev. Dr. C.T. Vivian,** known as Martin Luther King's "field general"; led sit-ins, boycotts and marches. Advocate of nonviolence. Baptist minister, and part of SCLC inner circle.

2006

- **Dr. Evelyn Brooks Higginbotham,** Victor S. Thomas Professor of History and of African American Studies at Harvard. President of the Association for the Study of African American Life. Received the 2014 National Humanities Medal from Obama.
- **The Rev. Dr. Wilma R. Johnson,** pastor of New Prospect Baptist Church. Known for her community outreach,

generosity, courage, and calm demeanor. Author and award recipient.
- **Dr. Julianne Malveaux,** economist, author, social commentator. Former president of Bennett College. Nationally broadcast radio host and syndicated columnist; author of numerous books.
- **Bishop Vashti Murphy McKenzie**, president of the National Council of Churches; first female bishop of the African Methodist Episcopal Church. Appointed by Obama to White House Commission of Faith-Based and Neighborhood Partnership. Author of six books.

2007

- **Dennis Archer,** author, lawyer, served 14 years as justice on the Michigan Supreme Court and as mayor of Detroit. First Black president of the American Bar Association. Taught at Detroit College of Law and Wayne State University Law School.
- **Taylor Branch**, ground-breaking historian and author of 10 books, including a seminal trilogy on the Civil Rights Movement; winner of Pulitzer Prize and National Book Critics Circle Award. Editor for *Harper's* and columnist for *Esquire*. Received MacArthur Foundation Fellowship and National Humanities Medal.

2008

- **The Rev. Charles Sherrod**, field secretary for the Student Nonviolent Coordinating Committee, led a campaign for 500 students in Albany. Worked at Southwest Georgia Project for Community Education, founded New Communities collective farm.

2009

- **The Rev. Dr. Cheryl Townsend Gilkes,** sociologist, womanist scholar, and Baptist minister. MacArthur Professor Emerita of African American Studies and Sociology at Colby College. Distinguished professor, community liaison, and research consultant, Howard Thurman Center. Author of the book *If It Wasn't for the Women.*
- **Clarence B. Jones,** author and lawyer, provided counsel and advice to Dr. King. Recipient of the Presidential Medal of Freedom. Chairman of the Spill the Honey Foundation. Smuggled out the "Letter from Birmingham Jail," and assisted in drafting the iconic "I Have a Dream" speech.

2010

- **The Rev. Dr. Calvin O. Butts III**, pastor, founder of Abyssinian Development Corporation. President, State University of New York College, Old Westbury.
- **Dr. Clayborne Carson**, Martin Luther King, Jr. Centennial Professor, emeritus, Stanford University. Published Dr. King's papers and then founded the MLK Research and Education Institute at Stanford. Received 2023 Freedom Award from the National Civil Rights Museum.

2011

- **Shirley Sherrod**, executive director, Southwest Georgia Project and vice president of development for New Communities at Cypress Pond. Worked with the Student

Nonviolence Coordinating Committee. Georgia state director of rural development.

2012

- **Diane Nash**, founding member of Student Nonviolence Coordinating Committee. Helped organize 1963 Birmingham desegregation and worked with Dr. King and SCLC during the Selma Voting Rights Campaign. Received Presidential Medal of Freedom.

2013

- **Donzaleigh Abernathy**, author, writer, director and producer, civil rights activist, award-winning actress in movies and television. Founding member of New Visions Foundation. Daughter of Jaunita and Ralph David Abernathy.
- **The Rev. Dr. Vincent Harding**, pastor, historian, scholar of American religion and society. Authored eight books about the Civil Rights Movement. Served as chairperson of Veterans for Hope, and a professor at Iliff School of Theology. Wrote speeches for Dr. King.
- **The Rev. Dr. James Lawson**, Expelled from faculty position at Vanderbilt for work in nonviolent resistance. Participated in Fellowship of Reconciliation, SCLC, Freedom Rides, and was influential in the founding of SNCC. Missionary to India and pastor.

2014

- **Rochelle Riley**, author, nationally syndicated columnist, *Detroit Free Press*, strong advocate for improved race relations. Won 2009 Pulitzer Prize and an Ida B. Wells Award.
- **John Seigenthaler**, journalist, writer, political figure, and prominent defender of the First Amendment. Editor of the *Tennessean* and founding editorial director of *USA Today*. Worked as Robert F. Kennedy's assistant, sent as government representative for the Freedom Riders.

2015

- **Harry Belafonte**, singer, actor and civil rights activist. Released 35 albums, appeared in 16 films. Received Grammy, Emmy, Tony, and humanitarian awards. Prominent figure and financial supporter of the Civil Rights Movement.
- **John Lewis**, U.S. representative for Georgia. Led Nashville sit-ins, Freedom Rides, Chairman of SNCC, planned March on Washington. Led march across Pettus Bridge on Bloody Sunday. Authored four award-winning graphic novels and received the Presidential Medal of Freedom.
- **The Rev. Al Sharpton**, civil rights and social justice activist, Baptist minister, radio talk show host, and TV personality. Ran for president, U.S. Senate, and mayor of New York City. Involved in many high-visibility events and provided George Floyd's eulogy.

From Slavery to Freedom: An American Odyssey

2016

- **Edwin Black**, award-winning international *New York Times* correspondent and author of books in 20 languages. Hosts weekly issues and history podcast with a companion YouTube channel. Speaks on human rights, corruption, corporate greed, governmental misconduct, and more.
- **Ernest Green,** one of the Little Rock Nine Black students who desegregated Little Rock (Arkansas) Central High School; first Black student to graduate there. Director of the A. Philip Randolph Fund, served as assistant secretary of labor under President Jimmy Carter.
- **Dr. Cornel West,** author, philosopher, theologian, political activist, social critic, and actor. Held academic appointments at Harvard, Yale, and Princeton. Ran for president for the Justice for All party.

2017

- **Jonathan Capehart,** Pulitzer Prize-winning journalist and member of the *Washington Post* editorial board. Hosts podcast "Capehart," anchors weekly live show "First Look," MSNBC contributor, anchor of "The Sunday Show with Jonathan Capehart." Commentator for "PBS NewsHour" on weekly segment "Brooks and Capehart."
- **The Honorable Johnny Ford**, first Black mayor of Tuskegee, Alabama; served eight nonconsecutive terms. Strategist for Robert F. Kennedy's campaign, director of Model Cities Program. President, National Council of Black Mayors.
- **Dr. Mae Jamison,** physician, engineer and astronaut. First African American woman to go into space. Author and

television spokesperson. Served in the Peace Corps and is fluent in Russian, Japanese, and Swahili.

2018

- **Dr. Michael Eric Dyson**, Baptist preacher, professor, author, and media personality. Taught at Princeton, Brown, Georgetown, and Vanderbilt. Won the Langston Hughes Medal, American Book Award, and two NAACP Image Awards.
- **Jemele Hill**, journalist, media personality, and writer. Sportswriter for *Detroit Free Press*, national columnist and on-air commentator at ESPN. Named Journalist of the Year by National Association of Black Journalists. Emmy award winner.

2019

- **Vernon E. Jordan, Jr.**, business executive, civil rights attorney. Part of President Clinton's transition team. Seriously wounded in assassination attempt. Managing director at an investment firm; served on numerous corporate boards.
- **Eugene Robinson**, Pulitzer Prize-winning columnist on politics and culture for the *Washington Post;* 30-year career includes correspondent on city, foreign, and style desks. Authored books on the splintering of Black America, affirmation of race, and Fidel Castro's final days.

From Slavery to Freedom: An American Odyssey

2020

- **The Rev. Dr. Kevin R. Murriel,** author, speaker and pastor of Cascade United Methodist Church in Atlanta. Studied ministry at Emory and Duke.
- **April Ryan,** reporter, author, and White House correspondent for *The Grio,* political contributor to MSNBC. Named Journalist of the Year by the National Association of Black Journalists. White House correspondent under five administrations.
- **Bankole Thompson,** *Detroit News* columnist, past editor of the *Michigan Chronicle* and host of "Redline with Bankole Thompson" weekly radio show on WDET. Wrote two books after sit-down interviews with President Obama, and was United Nations correspondent for Inter Press Service. Has interviewed numerous global leaders on geopolitical issues.

2021

- **Dr. Monique Couvson,** founded the National Black Women's Justice Institute. Author of six books, publications, and articles. President and CEO for Grantmakers for Girls of Color, with focus on improving education, justice, and economic status.
- **Patrisse Cullors,** co-founder of the Black Lives Matter Movement, artist and author. Executive director of BLM Global Network Foundation. Author of two highly acclaimed books. Appeared in documentary "Stay Woke," and produced "Resist," a 12-part YouTube series.

2022

- **LaTosha Brown**, social strategist, singer, songwriter and co-founder of Black Lives Matter. Received the White House Champion of Change Award and the Spirit of Democracy Award.
- **Brandan (BMike) Odums**, artist, activist, mentor. Through exhibitions and public artworks, elucidates the intersection of art and resistance. His studio was named one of the 50 best things to do by *Time Out* blog.
- **Yusef Salaam**, author, politician, motivational speaker. Member of New York City Council. One of the Exonerated Five wrongly accused of raping a woman in Central Park. Board Member of the Innocence Project. Received Lifetime Achievement Award from President Obama.

2023

- **Dr. Angela Davis**, feminist philosopher, activist, and author. Professor Emerita, UC Santa Cruz. Twice Communist Party's candidate for U.S. vice president.
- **Marley Dias** founded #1000BlackGirlBooks. Ambassador for NEA's Read Across America. Producer, Netflix's Bookmarks: *Celebrating Black Voices*.
- **Dr. Freeman Hrabowski**, author, educator, mathematician, president of University of Maryland, Baltimore County. Named to the President's Advisory Commission on Educational Excellence for African Americans.

2024

- **Dr. Tanisha C. Ford**, acclaimed writer, historian, and professor. Won NAACP Image Award for Outstanding Literary Work. Advises corporations on implementing equity in the workplace.
- **MC Lyte**, a pioneer of female rap, first to receive gold certification from the Recording Industry Association of America. Has collaborated with Queen Latifah, Janet Jackson, and Yo-Yo Ma. Performed at the White House. Received W.E.B. Du Bois Medal.
- **Dr. Rani Whitfield**, family and sports medicine physician in Baton Rouge. As the "Hip Hop Doc," he has made appearances on two BET series, the Chuck D radio shows, MSNBC, CNN, and more.

In Closing

Life, at best, is unpredictable. It takes many twists and turns, and rarely can we make plans that are not altered by time and circumstances. If we try too hard to attempt to plan the life that we live, we will be surprised at every turn and fail miserably. I could not have predicted the series of events that led to where we eventually arrived.

Meeting Norma, our marriage, having terrific children and wonderful grandchildren were not a result of careful planning. The choice of where to live, becoming friends with Dr. King and the Rev. Abernathy, was all part of a divine plan in our lives that extended far beyond our meager means to control it.

The chances that the only Black osteopathic physician in the entire South practiced in Albany, Georgia, and was my father's personal physician and friend, defies the laws of probability. Without this unpredicted, unplanned occurrence, I would not have become an osteopathic physician, nor would my children and grandchildren have followed me into the profession.

When Norma and I joined hands to take that first step on the moving walkway to freedom, we certainly did not plan on all that followed. I do not look back with regrets for the decisions that we made and those that were made for us, beyond our control.

There is a message here for us and for all who choose to read my life's stories. Don't argue with fate. Take life as it comes and make the most of what it gives you.

Nothing is impossible for those who believe and never give up on their dreams.

Here are my thoughts about:

Politics: Learning to navigate politics is a lifelong journey. Politics is not the most honorable thing that you will get involved in, but it's reality. Don't shy away, get involved and be part of the solution.

Friendship: If people see that you're motivated to do the right thing for the community that you come from, magic can happen. Look for people who believe in friendship. Build friendships with those who help keep your goals strongest for you. Do what you can do to make life better for them. Then when the opportunity comes, they will make it better for you. It does not take a lot of energy, a lot of effort, or a lot of formal education to develop friendships. There's nothing more important in life.

Perseverance: Essential to everything good. Don't give up. I had many doors slammed in my face because of my race or my color or my religion or whatever. I'm saying that you have to get beyond those things. Don't let them be barriers to what you want to do, what you're willing to sacrifice to do. Proceed as though the opportunities are waiting for you.If you may be hesitant to pursue your dreams, first tear down in your mind the blocks that you believe cannot be overcome. Don't let anything get in the way of what you want to do, who you want to be.

And never forget to give back. Generations will follow you and they will pattern their lives after what you did and how you did it. So, continue. Don't give up on your dreams. Continue, and you can succeed.

In Closing

The Osteopathic Profession: Holistic healthcare. This is what osteopathic medicine was created to do—treat the body, mind, and spirit. Roughly 150 years ago, Dr. Andrew Taylor Still created osteopathic medicine by looking at medicine through a different lens. A humane, holistic way of treating patients. He asked questions; he saw patients as whole people; he treated their condition regardless of color or gender. His teachings inspired followers, confused others, and angered them even more. The brightest minds came from across the world, you know—at first, they came to debunk his practice, but they immediately figured out he was the real deal and willing to share his knowledge with others who wanted to learn. Most stayed to learn, and later, they'd return home to practice the advanced health care that took into account social determinants of health, differences in gender, and allowances for medicinal treatments. While commonplace now, it was unheard of in an era of one-size-fits-all.

I practiced the principles of osteopathic medicine every day and soon discovered that there were people in and around Albany, Georgia, who needed not just medical care but emotional care, educational care, financial care, and opportunity care. And I did not have to put my practice aside to do that. Because of my osteopathic training, I had a better chance of addressing their issues.

And finally, The American Osteopathic Foundation (AOF)

The American Osteopathic Foundation (AOF) is a testament to the profession. It would not exist were it not for kind, charitable-minded people who support the profession through their generosity. I am immensely proud that donors have been so important in helping many, many students to avoid the pitfalls of segregation and discrimination and ignorance. Thank you. As a young medical student, at a time when I was feeling low, with no money and little prospects, the AOF provided me with a small loan. They believed I was a good risk. No interest, and we had years to pay it back. I cannot tell you how much that helped, and Norma and I never forgot what it meant to our family.

The AOF is nationally focused, so when Norma and I wrote our first book, we agreed that 100 percent of the proceeds would be used to start a scholarship award to support others who were struggling and possibly facing similar situations. Then, in 2019, the Heatherington Foundation for Innovation and Education in Healthcare announced they were going to add $1 million to the fund. They announced this on stage at AOF's annual Honors Gala and I had no idea this was coming, so I was speechless, and I cried right on stage in front of 1,000 people. It was a memorable moment, and ever since, I have had a special bond with Rita Forden, the Foundation's executive director.

Sometimes, when I dial Rita's number, my call goes to her assistant or her daughter's phone, a hazard of her daughter helping me update my phone over the summer. No matter what number I use, Rita always calls me back and is the person with whom I entrust this second book publishing. There are two leaders of the Heatherington Foundation—Jeff Heatherington is a businessman and son of a visionary osteopathic physician and community leader, and Robin "Rob" Richardson, D.O., is one of the nicest human beings this world has known. Rob always brings me cheese from his home state of Oregon whenever he passes through Michigan.

Presentation during AOF's Honors Gala 2019 (left to right: Martin Levine, DO; Barbara Ross-Lee, DO; Jeff Heatherington, LHD [Hon.]; Me; Rob Richardson, DO).

In Closing

It is important to note that every donor starts small. We give what we can, when we can. And that is going to change over time as life changes over time. There are unlimited opportunities for those who are willing to make just a little bit of sacrifice, especially to help the generations that follow them.

I want to congratulate all who have received scholarship funds from the AOF, and especially the Anderson Scholars. Now you can do what I did and others did before me: Give back to the next generation.

DO good. Be proud.

Vignettes

A consummate storyteller, Dr. William "Andy" Anderson's wisdom is almost completely contained in the parables of his life. If he drops by your office, if he's playing golf with you, if you share dinner, if you're at a meeting, Andy tells stories—intriguing stories, with flair and chuckles and a twinkle in his eye. Those illustrations enrich his public speaking and have put him in high demand for professional conferences, graduations, medical school lectures, civil rights history ceremonies, and more. These stories, many of which you now hold in your hands, are a brilliant tapestry of his life.

It is a life well-lived, a life of good example and courage, of catching opportunities and riding their winds wherever they took him. He would be the first to tell you to examine what he does in addition to what he says.

Here are some "wisdoms" and iconic quotes that are truly "Andy."

Wisdoms

Do something positive! Everyone should have ambition to do something because if you leave the world just as you found it, you might as well have stayed in your mother's womb. We don't need people to take up space. Do something positive to make this life a better place.

Bring people together! Because the dean of the MSU/COM gave me a free hand for nearly a quarter-century, I was able to bring to campus iconic civil rights leaders, many of whom were one or two generations removed from slavery. This series addressed the issues of segregation and discrimination, and its reputation spread throughout the United States. I am prouder of that than any other single opportunity that I had.

Build a strong foundation! My father's family were all motivated to get an education, recognizing that without it there was no future, especially for ex-slaves. There was no opportunity for them to advance without an education.

Be prepared for opportunities! Sometimes good things come to people unexpectedly, so be prepared. Be of the right mindset, in the event you are in the right place at the right time. Take advantage of opportunities that present themselves (like I did in the Navy when they offered to put me into hospital corpsman school).

Be the inspiration for others! You might ask how you can inspire other people. First, set an example by doing what others say cannot be done. If they see you succeed, and how you succeeded, then you can be an example the next generation can emulate. It's especially effec-

Vignettes

tive if they come from the same background as you. Second, you can advance an organization that promotes what you are doing to give those who follow you more opportunities. Make opportunities for generations yet to come. There are those who do not believe they could do it until they see it in you. Whenever you have the opportunity, encourage the next generation; life does not end with me or you. It goes on. And we would like to see that we have helped to motivate those who follow to exceed what we have done.

Be determined! Don't let anyone tell you what you cannot do. Once you get the training, work to succeed. If someone doesn't give you the opportunity to show you what you can do, do not accept this. Go back, go back, go back. Sometimes you can't wait for an opportunity to come your way. You have to make it or take it. Get in the way of your opportunity so it cannot get around you. Don't let them stop you because of your race, gender, color, creed, religion, culture, or sexual orientation. Those are artificial barriers.

Be humble! Do not forget that your life is not the beginning and end. We live in the midst of a generation where we are trying to motivate people to become better prepared for the future. So, the best way we can do that is to provide for them exposure to the past. If you do not know your past, you cannot predict your future. If you do not know your history, you cannot be a part of making a better history for those who follow you.

Begin sizing up your leaders! In every generation, in every race, every religion, every culture, there is a leader. Sometimes they're good leaders, sometimes they're not. Then how do we determine what's a good leader and what's a bad leader? See where they started and where they ended up. Intelligence is not limited by race, culture, religion, ethnicity, but in a large measure, it is measured by what you do and the positive difference you make.

Be determined (this is worth repeating)! Decide within yourself what you want to do, what you want to be, what kind of future you want to have. Each individual has the opportunity to set goals for themselves. No one can make those decisions for you. We have some great teachers, and we have some great leaders, but they cannot think for you, cannot act for you. They cannot be prepared for the hardships that you may be confronting. But set some objectives, some goals for yourself. I refer to them as the prize. Keep your eyes on the prize. It isn't original, but it stuck with me for the almost 100 years I've been here.

Special Recognition Awards

- **1962** – Rosa Parks Freedom Award, SCLC, Presented by Martin Luther King, Jr.
- **1982** – Walter F. Patenge Award of Public Service, MSU/COM
- **1983** – Focus and Impact Award for Leadership, Oakland University
- **1983** – Meritorious Service Award, MSU/COM
- **1987** – Alumni of the Year Award, Des Moines COM
- **1989** – Unsung Hero of the American Civil Rights Movement Award, Michigan
- **1989** – Martin Luther King, Jr. Service Recognition Award, Southfield
- **1990** – Doctor of Humane Letters (*honoris causa*), Ohio University COM
- **1990** – Phillips Medal of Public Service, Ohio University COM
- **1990** – Special Recognition Award, United States Army Tacoma

Special Recognition Awards

- **1991** – Civil Rights Pioneer, Students National Medical Association, Philadelphia COM
- **1991** – Leaders Award, Association of Black Osteopathic Medical Students, MSU/COM
- **1993** – City of Detroit Service Proclamation, Coleman A. Young, Mayor
- **1993** – State of Michigan Special Tribute, Senator Jackie Vaughn
- **1993** – Milestone Award for Outstanding Service, Albany, Georgia, NAACP
- **1994** – State of Georgia Proclamation, Zell Miller, Governor
- **1994** – Special Service Recognition Award, NYIT/COM
- **1994** – Orel F. Martin Distinguished Service Award, American College of Osteopathic Surgeons
- **1994** – Doctor of Laws (*honoris causa*), University of Osteopathic Medicine, Des Moines
- **1994** – Honorary Membership, Sigma Sigma Phi National Honorary Osteopathic Fraternity
- **1994** – Distinguished Public Service Award, Oklahoma State COM
- **1994** – Outstanding Health Communicator Award, Ohio COM
- **1995** – Power of One Award, Parklane Foundation, Kansas City
- **1995** – Doctor of Science in Osteopathy (*honoris causa*), Kirksville COM
- **1995** – State of Alabama Resolution, Alabama House of Representatives
- **1995** – Special Recognition Award, ACOOG
- **1995** – Special Recognition Award, Green Elementary School, Michigan
- **1995** – Honorary Commander in Chief, Association of Military Osteopathic Physicians and Surgeons

Special Recognition Awards

- **1995** – Honorary Life Membership, American Osteopathic Association
- **1996** – Inspirational Guidance Award, SNMA Chapter at NYIT/COM
- **1996** – Distinguished Service Award, VCOM
- **1997** – Certificate of Appreciation, American Osteopathic Association
- **1999** – Honorary Alumnus Award, Ohio University COM
- **1999** – Lifetime Achievement Award, National Osteopathic Medical Association
- **2000** – Commendation for Distinguished Service, University of North Texas COM
- **2002** – Distinguished Service Award, New York COM
- **2002** – Doctor of Science (*honoris causa*), Michigan State University
- **2003** – State of Michigan Special Recognition, State Representative Michael Murphy
- **2003** – Certificate of Special Congressional Recognition, Congressman Sanford Bishop
- **2008** – Lifetime Achievement Award, American Osteopathic Foundation
- **2020** – Robert A. Kistner Award, AACOM

Thank You For Reading My Book!

I appreciate your interest in my book and value your feedback as it helps me improve future versions of this book. I would appreciate it if you could leave your invaluable review on Amazon.com with your feedback.
Thank you!

www.ingramcontent.com/pod-product-compliance
Lightning Source LLC
LaVergne TN
LVHW011415080426
835512LV00005B/72